approach
to classification

FOR STUDENTS OF LIBRARIANSHIP

DEREK LANGRIDGE

LINNET BOOKS & CLIVE BINGLEY

Library of Congress Cataloging in Publication Data

Langridge, Derek Wilton.
   Approach to classification.

   Includes bibliographies.
   1. Classification—Books. I. Title.
Z696.L26   025.4   72–8181
ISBN 0-208-01184-6

**To the M Sc class of 1971, Instituto Brasileiro de Bibliografia
e Documentação, Rio de Janeiro**

First published 1973 by Clive Bingley Ltd
This edition simultaneously published in the USA by
Linnet Books, an imprint of Shoe String Press Inc,
995 Sherman Avenue, Hamden, Connecticut 06514
Printed in Great Britain
© Derek Langridge 1973

approach
to classification

FOR STUDENTS OF LIBRARIANSHIP

CONTENTS

page

Preface 7

Prologue: A day in the life of Everyman and his wife 9

PART 1 : Classification in general 13

PART 2 : Classification of knowledge 33

PART 3 : Library classification : the elements 47

PART 4 : Library classification : the schemes 83

PART 5 : Classification and subject indexing 107

Epilogue 118

Index 119

PREFACE

At one time it was fashionable to write about classification and cataloguing as if they were mutually exclusive subjects. Nowadays it is more common to distinguish between subject work on the one hand, author, title and descriptive cataloguing on the other. This is very right and proper, but there is still a place for the discussion of classification in its own right: it is a process that can be described without taking detailed account of specific ends to which it may be devoted.

In this book I have made no attempt to explain the whole subject of indexing: I have merely indicated the role of classification in this activity. Nor am I competing with any of the modern textbooks on library classification. This introduction is more elementary in that it gives only an outline of the subject; more comprehensive in that it deals with all aspects of classification. It is impossible to understand library classification properly without being aware of the full import of this pervasive activity.

One specific task I have set myself is to act as a guide through the increasing confusions of terminology. There has been quite unnecessary proliferation of terms during the last decade, and this more than anything else makes the subject appear more difficult to the beginner than it really is. I have emphasised the terminology of Ranganathan since it is widely used in modern writings and is by far the most precise and consistent. The many important terms are capitalised throughout the text. As in most subjects, there are some matters of near certainty in classification, some of opposing schools of thought or even more divided opinion. I have tried to make these distinctions clear.

As far as possible I have dealt with one major idea on each page of the text, summarised in the capitalised heading. Further readings are indicated for each part. These vary enormously in difficulty and their inclusion does not mean that they are necessarily suitable for beginners. They are available if and when the reader wishes to increase his knowledge of a particular aspect of the subject.

My debts to other people, both living and dead, are inevitably extensive; but I would like to thank in particular my colleagues at the Polytechnic of North London, my fellow members of the Classification Research Group, my students past and present in England, USA, and Brazil, the staff of the DRTC in Bangalore and Dr S R Ranganathan, the great pioneer of modern library classification.

DEREK LANGRIDGE

June 1972

PROLOGUE
A day in the life of Everyman and his wife

John Brown's waking thought was the first of countless acts of classification that he performed every day. Before he could do anything he had to decide whether it was a working day or a holiday. On holidays he went back to sleep; on working days he moved quickly to the bathroom. This had been the easiest room in the house to organise by virtue of another elementary classification : His and Hers. His razor, brush, after-shave lotion were in one cabinet, Her shampoos, powders and creams in another; His facecloth and soap on the left side of the hand-basin, Hers on the right; His bath towel blue, Hers pink. John Brown was an industrial consultant. More than most people he was conscious that the major problem of economics is how we use our time. Even the few minutes gained by a tidy bathroom he regarded as a significant part of his efficiency.

Returning to the bedroom he went first to the wardrobe to decide on his outer clothing for the day. This was facilitated by the order of items on the rail. They were roughly in order of weight and size: heavy overcoats on the left, followed by lighter coats, raincoat, formal suits, waistcoats, sports jackets and jerkins.

Shirts were laid out on shelves at right and left of the wardrobe. They were classified by no less than three different principles : formal or informal; thick or thin; and colour. Since Mr Brown was a business man the question of formality was paramount. Accordingly his formal shirts were all on the right hand shelves, informal ones on the left. (The choice of side was, of course, making unconscious use of one of the most deeply ingrained classifications in the human mind : right for anything associated with correctness, left for all deviations.) On each side, the light shirts occupied the higher shelves, the heavy occupied the lower. Within each of these groups there were four colour divisions: red and yellow; green and brown; blue and grey; and white. As an industrial consultant Mr

Brown had some knowledge of psychology and was thus more or less conscious of the significance of this colour classification. Red and yellow were the 'hot' colours for occasions when he wished to express his driving energy or high spirits; green and brown were relaxed, pastoral; blue and grey were cool and reticent; white was the ideal for all occasions.

With similar principles used in the arrangement of all his clothing, Mr Brown was able to dress quickly and appropriately for his mood and the day's programme. Meanwhile his wife prepared breakfast, aided by equally efficient organisation in the kitchen. Items of food were classified first according to their need for protection from air, heat and dust: milk, meat and eggs in the refrigerator; bread and biscuits in air-tight containers; packaged items in various cabinets. The refrigerator was divided into compartments according to the degree of freezing required; biscuits were in separate tins for sweet and dry; packets and bottles were grouped as beverages, cereals, preserves and condiments. Further cabinets and drawers separated table-cloths, cutlery and crockery.

Mr Brown's schedule allowed time for a quick perusal of the morning paper. This was his first contact of the day with a classification not of his own making. The front page was dedicated to the most startling news of the day, back page to its overflow. The first few inside pages were for politics, divided into home and overseas, followed by sections for arts and fashions. The centre spread contained editorial comment and readers' letters. The second half began with educational items and continued with business activities and the explicitly 'classified advertisements'—business posts, educational posts and secretarial posts. The issue finished with the day's sport.

As Mr Brown left the house, his wife began her day's work by washing up the breakfast things. Being as orderly in her habits as her husband, she began by arranging the utensils in neat groups beside the sink—glasses, cups, saucers, plates and cutlery—for washing in that order. Her motto, handed down by her mother and her grandmother before that, was 'A place for everything and everything in its place'—the epitome of practical classification.

Like many other housewives, Mrs Brown enjoyed listening to

the radio while she worked. On this particular morning she was surprised by the title of a song by Jerome Kern that she had not heard before: 'A woman is only a woman, but a good cigar is a smoke'. Her reaction, not surprisingly, was 'If he feels that way, I hope the smoke gets in his eyes'. A more conscious knowledge of classification would have helped Mrs Brown to see that the joke is not against women. In fact, it says that while a cigar is merely one species of the genus ' smokes ', woman is unique, *sui generis.*

Later in the morning Mrs Brown went to the local supermarket for her week's shopping. Here she was aided in the quick and easy selection of goods by the system of classification used in their display. Most of the store was devoted to food and drink, but there were separate counters for pharmaceuticals and household cleaning materials. In the food section two special groups of consumers were catered for: babies and dogs. For the rest, there was a major distinction between fresh and tinned food. The main sequence was arranged in relation to meals: meat and fish were grouped with related items such as condiments, stuffing, and cooking foil; bread, cakes and biscuits with the raw materials for their making; milk products were all together, as were beverages and the closely associated sugar. Had Mrs Brown been classification conscious she might have wondered why matches were next to disinfectants and eggs on the same counter as bread. Otherwise, the whole arrangement was simple, obvious and helpful.

The fruit of Mrs Brown's efficiency was a free afternoon and she decided to go to the cinema. At the entrance she was accosted by a girl and boy asking if she would take them in since the film was classified as AA, meaning that it could be shown only to those over 14 or accompanied by an adult. (The other classes are U—fit for showing to anyone, A—a caution that the viewer might find something objectionable, and X—for those over 18).

Two hours later she emerged from the cinema, just too late to save a young woman from stepping off the kerb in front of a car. She turned out to be a French *au pair* who had only recently arrived in the country. She was not yet used to the fact that our classification of traffic-flow in England is different from the rest of the world, so that vehicles on her side of the road would be approaching from the right and not from the left. Fortunately, the car had only given her a glancing blow, but she was sufficiently shaken by the accident to need hospital attention. Mrs Brown had time to spare and offered to accompany the girl.

The hospital, like all institutions, depended on a variety of classifications for its functions. Patients were first divided into those who were detained and those who merely visited. A further classification divided the hospital's activities according to kinds of illness or treatment into Surgical, Medical, Pediatrics, Geriatrics, Obstetrics, etc. Within each division separate wards were allocated to men and women, for obvious reasons.

After the exertions of the day, Mr and Mrs Brown spent their evening quietly watching television and listening to the radio. Here again they found principles of classification applied to the allocation of programmes. Television was divided explicitly according to whether the producing company was BBC or ITV, and less explicitly into three degrees of popular appeal: ITV, BBC1, and BBC2. Radio programmes have four classes, apparently aimed respectively at youth, women, music-lovers and the homely. These four classes are definitely not mutually exclusive—a term that will be explained in the more technical pages that follow.

This is obviously a stylised and idealised account of Everyman. In practice most people are not as orderly as the Browns, and the failures of classification are as likely to be in evidence as the successes. There is no question, however, of the pervasiveness of classification in all our activities.

PART 1
CLASSIFICATION IN GENERAL

CLASSIFICATION IS WITH YOU ALWAYS

That most people are unaware of how much classifying they do is merely an indication of its fundamental nature. Their condition is similar to that of the famous character in a Molière play who is surprised to discover that he has been talking prose all his life.

Without classification there could be none of the human thought, action and organisation that we know. Classification transforms isolated and incoherent sense impressions into recognisable objects and recurring patterns. An English psychologist, Patrick Meredith, has written: 'A great deal of the art of learning consists in regularising one's habits of classification'. The American philosopher John Dewey even suggested at one point that 'Knowledge *is* classification'. This may not be a very accurate definition of knowledge, but it does effectively emphasise the significant role of classification.

SIMPLE CLASSIFICATIONS FACILITATE EVERYDAY LIFE

It is obvious that a whole host of simple classifications are used by Mr Brown and those with whom he has regular contact. At this level classification is largely unconscious and uncomplicated. It includes not only things and actions, but also persons. We all have rough and ready classifications of people based on tradition and personal experience. For example, we have different expectations of thin people and fat people, of tall people and short people; and some men, at least, tend to think of women as falling into three classes of blonde, brunette and redhead.

In one day the Browns encountered many examples of classification by various institutions—newspapers, business, welfare, local and central government. These differed from their own in that they were mainly quite consciously applied, even though some were as simple as theirs.

SOCIAL ORGANISATION REQUIRES MANY CLASSIFICATIONS RANGING FROM SIMPLE TO COMPLEX

Many classifications are for the arrangement of physical objects. These may be fairly simple and obvious, as in a supermarket, or they may be more complex and require expert knowledge in construction and use, as in a factory store of spare parts. The late Edward G Brisch was an industrial consultant who specialised in classifying stores. He arranged parts by such characteristics as material, shape and size. By thus bringing appropriate order to such collections he was able to improve significantly the efficient operation of firms. Other examples of objects needing detailed classification are exhibits in museums, paintings and sculpture in art galleries, and animals in zoos.

Though the two are related, we may distinguish between classification for the arrangement of objects and classification of ideas. Generally speaking the latter is more complex and more difficult.

THERE MAY BE MANY WAYS OF CLASSIFYING THE SAME OBJECTS OR IDEAS

People are the best example. We have already noted that everyone has his own rough and ready classification of people, but there are many more. We can classify people by physical characteristics, such as height, weight, colour or age; by economic characteristics, such as rich and poor; by political characteristics, such as liberal and conservative; by social characteristics such as conventional and unconventional; by educational characteristics, religious character-istics, philosophical characteristics and so on. There is no end to the possibilities.

The most interesting question of classification is whether there is any fundamental division of people. Whether there is one classification from this large range which helps us most in under-standing people (apart from the very obvious division of the sexes).

The ancient world produced a fourfold classification of people into the sanguine, the choleric, the phlegmatic and the melancholic. The modern world has adopted Carl Jung's division into extrovert (turned to the outer world) and introvert (turned to the inner world). Jung himself further divided each type according to the predominance in the person of thinking, feeling, sensation or intui-tion. Less well-known is the work of Adolphe Ferrière who spent fifty years in research and produced a broad classification of twelve human types with further subdivisions of each. The most interesting feature of this classification is that it corresponds closely to the most ancient classification of types known to us—the signs of the Zodiac in Astrology. Dr Ferrière in his book, *Psychological types,* pointed out that the actual symbols used in the Zodiac showed an astonishing intuition on the part of the primitive peoples who chose them, and 'Just as the intuition of the alchemists paved the way for many of the scientific data of chemistry, so the astrologists intuitively prepared many of the data of scientific typology'.

There have also been various attempts to establish broad classes of man by physical characteristics, including types of hand.

MAN MAKES CLASSIFICATIONS, HE DOES NOT DISCOVER THEM

Some writers have implied in the past that there is an absolute classification of the world waiting to be discovered. This misrepresents the facts, since the most we can say with certainty is that the structure of our minds is responsible for our seeing the world in certain ways.

The status of classifications is well expressed by the American poet Robinson Jeffers in his poem ' Monument '.

' Erase the lines: I pray you not to love classifications:
The thing is like a river, from source to sea-mouth
One flowing life. . . . The classifications
Are mostly a kind of *memoria technica,* use it but don't be fooled.'

The limitations of the human mind are expressed very simply and forcefully in the nursery rhyme:

Humpty Dumpty sat on the wall,
Humpty Dumpty had a great fall,
All the King's horses and all the King's men,
Couldn't put Humpty together again.

Humpty Dumpty symbolises the unity of existence. Since the Fall of Man (another symbolic way of referring to the human state) Will-power (the King's horses) and Intellect (the King's men) are incapable of seeing this world whole as it really is.

THE DISTINCTION BETWEEN NATURAL AND ARTIFICIAL CLASSIFICATION IS IMPORTANT IN SOME CIRCUMSTANCES

In his pursuit of knowledge, Man has looked for those classifications that are most fundamental. Scientists favour classes in which the members have the largest possible number of features in common. For example, zoologists classify animals according to structural similarities. By this method whales belong to the same class (mammals) as horses, cows, rabbits and mice. The layman would be more inclined to think of whales as belonging to the same class as fishes because they both live in water, but this proves to be a more or less isolated characteristic—whales and fishes do not have much else in common. The first kind of classification is known as *natural*, the second as artificial. For the scientist seeking maximum knowledge of the world this distinction is important, but for many other applications of classification it is not. The farmer is not trying to produce knowledge but food. His major division of animals would put horses and cows in the useful class and rabbits and mice in the pest class. That zoologists classify all four as mammals is of no interest to him. Similarly he wouldn't think of whales as animals at all, since he wouldn't expect to see them either keeping his cows company or eating his corn. The fishing industry, on the other hand, would regard whales as coming within their province, since the activities aimed at making use of whales are similar to those aimed at fishes.

CHOICE OF CLASSIFICATION IS ALWAYS RELATED TO PURPOSE

It is now obvious that we can have many classifications. There is therefore no question of judging any particular classification as being right or wrong. It can only be more or less good for its purpose, though some classifications may serve more purposes than others.

The relativity of classification is immortalised in the following exchange between Alice and the Caterpillar (Lewis Carroll: *Alice's adventures in wonderland* chapter V).

'Serpent!' screamed the Pigeon.

'I'm *not* a serpent!' said Alice indignantly. 'Let me alone!'

'Serpent, I say again!' repeated the Pigeon, but in a more subdued tone, and added with a kind of sob, 'I've tried every way, and nothing seems to suit them!'

'I haven't the least idea what you're talking about,' said Alice.

'I've tried the roots of trees, and I've tried banks, and I've tried hedges,' the Pigeon went on, without attending to her; 'but those serpents! There's no pleasing them!'

Alice was more and more puzzled, but she thought there was no use in saying anything more till the Pigeon had finished.

'As if it wasn't trouble enough hatching the eggs,' said the Pigeon; 'but I must be on the look-out for serpents night and day! Why, I haven't had a wink of sleep these three weeks!'

'I'm very sorry you've been annoyed,' said Alice, who was beginning to see its meaning.

'And just as I'd taken the highest tree in the wood,' continued the Pigeon, raising its voice to a shriek, 'and just as I was thinking I should be free of them at last, they must needs come wriggling down from the sky! Ugh, Serpent!'

'But I'm *not* a serpent, I tell you!' said Alice. 'I'm a — I'm a —'.

'Well! *What* are you?' said the Pigeon. 'I can see you're trying to invent something!'

' I—I'm a little girl,' said Alice, rather doubtfully, as she remembered the number of changes she had gone through that day.

'A likely story indeed!' said the Pigeon in a tone of the deepest contempt. ' I've seen a good many little girls in my time, but never *one* with such a neck as that! No, no! You're a serpent; and there's no use denying it. I suppose you'll be telling me next that you never tasted an egg!'

' I *have* tasted eggs, certainly,' said Alice, who was a very truthful child; ' but little girls eat eggs quite as much as serpents do, you know.'

' I don't believe it,' said the Pigeon; ' but if they do, why, then, they're a kind of serpent, that's all I can say.'

This was such a new idea to Alice, that she was quite silent for a minute or two, which gave the Pigeon the opportunity of adding, ' You're looking for eggs, I know *that* well enough; and what does it matter to me whether you're a little girl or a serpent?'

THE PURPOSE OF CLASSIFICATION IN LIBRARIES IS TO ORGANISE KNOWLEDGE AS EMBODIED IN BOOKS AND OTHER MEDIA

Librarianship consists of the selection, organisation and dissemination of knowledge presented in various physical forms. The most important technique used in this organisation is classification. Since books have been for long the most important medium for communicating knowledge, the term BIBLIOGRAPHIC CLASSIFICATION is often used as a synonym for LIBRARY CLASSIFICATION. Either term implies the use of classification not only for the arrangement of stock on the shelves (sometimes called SHELF CLASSIFICATION) but also for the arrangement of subject entries in catalogues, indexes and bibliographies.

ORGANISATION OF KNOWLEDGE is the most comprehensive term expressing the library function served by classification. It indicates the ability not only to pinpoint specific and precisely defined items of information, but also to demonstrate the complete range of subjects available in the library and their relations to each other. This is a very important educational function of libraries, and one that has been somewhat overlooked in modern studies of classification. It is significant that where pre-war writers did use the term Organisation of Knowledge, modern writers have mostly substituted terms like INFORMATION RETRIEVAL or INFORMATION STORAGE AND RETRIEVAL.

It is possible to have isolated units of *information,* but the term *knowledge* implies organisation. Their relationship is suggested in T S Eliot's lines:

' Where is the Life we have lost in living?
Where is the wisdom we have lost in knowledge?
Where is the knowledge we have lost in information?'

Of course, unless we do also provide for specific information retrieval the users will add to these lines ' Where is the information we have lost in the library?'

LIBRARY CLASSIFICATION DEPENDS ON MORE FUNDAMENTAL STUDIES

Fundamental study of classification is closely related to the study of meaning and definition. Contributions are made in different ways by psychologists, linguists and philosophers.

Psychologists are concerned with the process of classification as it occurs in the human mind. They investigate its development in children and its role in all thinking and learning. Linguistics and semantics deal with meanings, definitions and classifications embodied in particular languages. These are all scientific studies in that they observe, describe and make generalisations about human behaviour.

Philosophers, on the other hand, are concerned with the nature of these activities—with what precisely we mean when we talk of meaning, definition or classification.

' CONCEPT ' IS THE MOST FUNDAMENTAL TERM IN ALL STUDIES RELATED TO CLASSIFICATION

It is important to distinguish between concepts and words. Concepts are *expressed in* words but they are *not identical with* words. For example, an Englishman will use the word ' horse ' where a Frenchman uses the word ' cheval ' for exactly the same concept. It is also possible to have a concept of something for which there is no word, or for which we do not know the word.

Many, though not all, concepts are class-concepts. That is to say they are our *idea* of a particular group of objects. In library classification we are concerned with concepts rather than with the objects themselves.

Understanding a class-concept can be demonstrated in two ways —by the ability to say whether or not a given object belongs to the class, or by the ability to describe the properties (or characteristics) by virtue of which it does belong. I may be said to have grasped the concept of horse if I understand the word ' horse '. I demonstrate this *either* by selecting a horse from a group of animals while rejecting a cow, sheep or goat, *or* by saying that a horse is a hoofed mammal etc (*ie* by defining the word ' horse ').

CLASS MEMBERSHIP MUST BE DISTINGUISHED FROM CLASS INCLUSION

The two aspects of a class-concept give rise to the terms ' class membership ' and ' class inclusion '. The members of a class are the *individual objects* of which it is composed. The term ' class inclusion ', on the other hand, is restricted to narrower *classes* included in a broader class. For example, the members of the class Man are Socrates, Shakespeare, Groucho Marx etc; the sub-classes of the class man are rich men, poor men, beggar men, thieves etc.

Scientific knowledge is concerned solely with classes, but in the humanities the emphasis is very much on individuals—writers and their books, musicians and their compositions, painters and their paintings. Library classification is therefore interested in class membership as well as class inclusion.

The DENOTATION of a term is the members of the class represented by that term. Related terms are not used consistently by logicians. EXTENSION is often used as synonymous with denotation, but sometimes, more usefully, to mean all the narrower classes included within a broader class (or all the species of a genus). These narrower classes will be based on properties of the broader class (*eg* the classes Englishmen, Frenchmen etc, are based on the property of Nationality). There are two terms used to refer to properties of a class. CONNOTATION means the set of properties (characteristics or attributes) which define the term for the class. INTENSION is sometimes used with the same meaning—sometimes amplified to ' conventional intension '. It may also be used to mean *all* the properties shared in common by members of a class—sometimes called the ' objective intension '; or all the properties present in the mind of a person who refers to the class—sometimes called the ' subjective intension '.

We could illustrate the use of these terms in relation to the class ' Rose '.

Denotation=Each and every rose that exists, did exist or will exist.

Extension=Every *kind* of rose, damask rose, tea rose, etc.

26

Connotation (or conventional intension)=the *small number* of properties that constitute the botanist's definition of rose (*ie essential* properties).

Objective intension=All the properties shared by all roses, *eg* Colour within a range of red, white, pink and yellow, sweet perfume varying in intensity, etc.

Subjective intension=Any individual person's response to the word 'rose'. As well as properties in the objective intension this might include recollections of literary works—'By any other name', 'Oh rose! thou art sick', rose red cities half as old as time; song titles—Rose of Washington Square, Rose Room, Roses of Picardy; girls called Rose, *Cider with Rosie;* rose windows; watering-cans etc.

THE BASIC RULES FOR CLASSIFICATION ARE TO BE FOUND IN LOGIC

Logic is concerned with correct procedures in reasoning. Thus, although it is normally regarded as a branch of philosophy, it is applicable to all disciplines that attempt to reach conclusions through the examination of evidence.

The unit for analysis in logic is the judgment or proposition (*ie* what is expressed by a sentence when a statement is made). It consists of a subject and predicate, as in 'All men (subject) are mortal (predicate)'. Logic must distinguish the various *kinds of terms* (a synonym for concepts in this context) and for this prescribes the basic rules of classification. Though a distinction is sometimes made between classification (the grouping of objects into classes) and logical division (dividing a class into sub-classes), they are really only two aspects of one activity, and in library work it is normal to use the word classification to cover both. The textbooks of logic give the following basic rules of classification (or logical division).

1 The characteristic (principle) of division must produce at least two classes. For example, the characteristic of sex when applied to the class of ' persons in general ' does produce at least two classes, but not if applied to the class of ' mothers ' who are by definition all female.

2 Only one principle of division must be used at a time to produce mutually exclusive classes. (If they overlap then it is impossible to be certain which class any given object belongs to. This error is known as cross-classification, and is one of the most serious that can occur in library work.) Two of the many characteristics we could apply to persons are age and sex (*NB* One should avoid referring to this act of division as ' Persons broken down by age and sex '). If both characteristics are applied at once we should have the following classification:

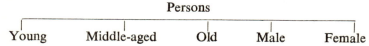

Persons

Young   Middle-aged   Old   Male   Female

28

where 'young men', for example, could be placed in one of two classes; to avoid this 'cross-classification' the characteristics must be applied one at a time, in whatever order suits the purpose of the exercise. For example:

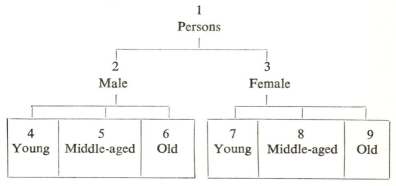

In this classification it is clear that 'young men' must go in box no 4 (box no 2 is the general class of all male persons irrespective of age).

3 The sub-classes must be completely exhaustive of their parent class (otherwise we are left with an unknown element).

4 In dividing a class successively into smaller and smaller subdivisions, no step of division must be omitted (otherwise there will be items that we cannot classify properly). This rule is sometimes referred to as the principle of modulation.

THERE ARE LIMITATIONS TO THE USE OF LOGICAL DIVISION FOR LIBRARY PURPOSES

The production of mutually exclusive classes is an ideal which is only sometimes attained with the very precise definitions of science. It is only science that attempts precise definitions. Language normally depends on a variety of meanings that are constantly changing. In most subjects it is therefore not easy to establish mutually exclusive classes.

It is also difficult to be sure that a set of sub-classes do in fact completely exhaust the parent class—both difficult to be certain which classes already exist and difficult to predict what further classes may be discovered or created in future.

It is even more difficult to observe the fourth rule since there is nothing absolute about the number of steps necessary to divide a given class into all its subdivisions. This again is because we *make* classifications rather than discover them. For librarians the number of steps taken to divide a given class will depend on how the subject is written about.

The most serious limitation to logical division is that it is concerned with only one kind of relationship—that of a thing and its kinds, known in scientific contexts as *genus and species*. In library classification we are concerned with many other relationships.

One which is sometimes confused with logical division is partition—division of a whole into its parts. For example, if I divide countries into those with a hot climate and those with a cold climate I am performing logical division and showing a genus/species relationship. But if I divide England into its counties I am merely showing a whole/part relationship. A hot country is obviously a *kind* of country and Surrey is equally obviously *not* a *kind* of England, but a part.

Other relationships will be dealt with later in this text.

READINGS FOR PART ONE

1 *Classification in social organisation*

Bliss, H E: *The organisation of knowledge and the system of the sciences.* New York, Holt, 1929 (chapters 1-4).

Kyle, B: 'Classification in the school curriculum' *in* Foskett, D J and Palmer, B I *(eds) The Sayers memorial volume,* Library Association, 1961.

2. *Classification of people*

Ferrière, Adolphe: *Psychological types and the stages of man's development,* translated by Wyatt Rawson. Heinemann, 1958.

Gettings, Fred: *The book of the hand.* Hamlyn, 1965.

Jung, C G: *Psychological types.* Routledge & Kegan Paul, 1926.

MacNiece, Louis: *Astrology.* Aldus Books, 1964 (chapter 3 ' The signs of the zodiac ').

Mayo, Jeff: *Teach yourself astrology.* English Universities Press, 1964 (chapter 4 ' The 12 signs : psychological types ').

Sheldon, W H: *The varieties of human physique.* New York, Harper, 1940.

Sheldon, W H: *The varieties of temperament.* New York, Harper, 1942.

3 *The analysis of classification (in psychology, linguistics, semantics and philosophy)*

Collingwood, R G: *An essay on philosophical method.* Oxford University Press, 1933.

Meredith, Patrick: *Learning, remembering and knowing.* English Universities Press, 1961.

Thomson, Robert: *The psychology of thinking.* Penguin, 1959.

Wilson, John: *Thinking with concepts.* Cambridge University Press, 1966.

4 *Classification in logic*

Mellone, S H: *An introductory textbook of logic.* Blackwood, 19th ed 1950.

Stebbing, S: *A modern elementary logic.* Methuen, 5th ed 1952.

PART 2
CLASSIFICATION OF KNOWLEDGE

WHAT IS A SUBJECT?

This question could be answered variously with such examples as:

1 Mice.

2 The care of pet mice.

3 Population characteristics of house mice living in English corn ricks: density relationships.

4 Zoology.

The first three differ only in degree of complexity. They are all similar in that they refer to PHENOMENA of the world which constitute the subject matter of knowledge.

Zoology, on the other hand, is quite different. It does not name some phenomenon of the world that we observe but a DISCIPLINE, or branch of knowledge.

We must therefore distinguish clearly between the division of the universe into kinds of phenomena, and the division of knowledge into kinds of knowledge.

PHILOSOPHERS INVESTIGATE THE KINDS OF KNOWLEDGE

We have already seen that one and the same set of objects or ideas may be classified in different ways for different purposes. It should therefore come as no surprise that philosophers use various principles for dividing knowledge. For example, it may be divided according to the knower, as in the threefold division of animal knowledge, human knowledge and divine knowledge. It may be divided according to the means of knowing, such as the faculties of sense, reason, memory and intuition. It may be divided according to purposes such as practical, intellectual, entertainment and spiritual.

The modern philosophical writings of greatest relevance to library classification are those by philosophers of education. In particular they are concerned with identifying the fundamental forms of knowledge as a basis for curriculum design.

FUNDAMENTAL DISCIPLINES PROVIDE THE PRIMARY DIVISION OF KNOWLEDGE FOR EDUCATIONAL PURPOSES

Only in the mystical vision is life apprehended as a whole. For the rest, as St Paul says, 'we see in part'. All human knowledge is partial knowledge and our different approaches to the world are reflected in distinct FORMS OF KNOWLEDGE or FUNDAMENTAL DISCIPLINES. There is a considerable degree of agreement among modern philosophers as to what these are.

Paul Hirst, Professor of Education at Cambridge, uses four criteria for defining these forms: the concepts used, the logical structure, the methodology and the means of testing findings. With these criteria he distinguishes eight forms: Mathematics, Physical science, Human science, History, Moral knowledge, Art, Religion and Philosophy. Science and Art in particular have many subdivisions such as Physics, Chemistry, Music and Architecture. In practice the word 'discipline' is used indiscriminately to refer to any systematic body of knowledge and it is therefore helpful to use 'fundamental discipline' when referring to the major divisions of knowledge.

Professor Hirst also recognises two other modes of organising knowledge. One he calls fields of knowledge, in which knowledge from various forms is collected around a central object or interest, such as Power or the European mind. The other he calls practical theories. Unlike the other two, which are organisations for the development of understanding itself, this last is aimed at practice. Medicine, Engineering, Education, and Librarianship itself are all examples, where knowledge is drawn from various disciplines to be used in formulation of principles for action.

THE UNITY OF KNOWLEDGE IS A CONTROVERSIAL TOPIC

Agreement on the division of knowledge into disciplines does not mean agreement on the unity of knowledge. There is no guarantee that the various bodies of knowledge fit together to form a complete and comprehensive picture of reality. The American philosopher, J H Randall, has made the useful distinction between the World *for* Knowledge (which is assumed to be one) and the World *of* Knowledge (which may remain many). At the extremes both mystic and scientist affirm the unity of the universe, but we continue to have quite distinct bodies of knowledge *about* the universe.

Those who set out to construct classification schemes for knowledge must explore as far as they can the details of relationship between the various forms of knowledge. This is much easier between the subdivisions of a fundamental discipline, such as Science, than between the fundamental disciplines themselves. It is easier to analyse the relationships between Physics, Chemistry, and Biology than those between Science, Philosophy, History and Art.

Apart from these subject considerations, there are others relating to different cultures and different epochs. It is by no means certain that the knowledge of the major cultures of India, China and the West can be integrated; and within Western culture, at least, there are distinct epochs in which the pattern of knowledge varies enormously.

SCIENTISTS INVESTIGATE THE KINDS OF PHENOMENA WITHIN PARTICULAR DISCIPLINES

Unlike philosophers, scientists are not concerned with the whole of knowledge. Each scientist is a specialist, directing his attention to a limited range of phenomena. Each science must make its own classification within those limits. Zoology gives us a classification of animals, Botany of plants, Geology of rocks, Medicine of diseases, Sociology of human groups, and so on. Library classification must make use of every scientific system that exists. This does not mean that library classification is a mere compilation from such sources. There is a great deal more to be done, as we shall see later.

In the case of a developing science there may be no consensus of opinion among specialists on the classification of phenomena within its scope. Here the maker of a library classification will be forced to choose between alternative possibilities.

THE MOST GENERAL CLASSES OF PHENOMENA ARE KNOWN AS CATEGORIES

In everyday use the terms 'class' and 'category' are virtually synonymous. In classification we reserve the term 'category' for the most general classes of phenomena. The chief categories of phenomena are common experience. Everyone is familiar with the category of things (or entities), roughly corresponding to the grammatical distinction of concrete nouns; with the category of activities (represented by verbs); and the category of properties (qualities or attributes) such as colour, shape, size and weight.

From Aristotle onwards, philosophers have considered the nature and number of the fundamental categories of existence. The fact that there is no general agreement need not worry the makers of library classifications. The question for them is not whether a given set of categories is *right*, but whether it *works efficiently*.

RELATIONSHIPS BETWEEN PHENOMENA ARE ALSO IMPORTANT IN THE CLASSIFICATION OF KNOWLEDGE

Categories are one major element in modern classification theory for the analysis of phenomena. Another important element is the concept of RELATIONSHIPS between categories. There is a relationship between a thing and its properties, a thing and its actions, a thing and the actions performed on it, and so on.

In addition, we have already seen that logic discusses the relationship of a genus and its species (relationships *within* a given category). The genus is said to be *superordinate* to its species; the species *subordinate* to the genus; and the species of a genus *coordinate* with each other.

We have also seen that this relationship is sometimes confused with the relationship of a thing to its parts, or of a class to its members.

CLASSIFICATION SYSTEMS FOR KNOWLEDGE MAY THEMSELVES BE CLASSIFIED ACCORDING TO PURPOSE

A complete map of any area of knowledge, showing all its concepts and their relationships, is known as a CLASSIFICATION SCHEME or SYSTEM. Such schemes may be designed for different purposes and a useful classification of these purposes is given by E C Richardson. He divides systems first into the theoretical and the practical. Theoretical fall into three classes:

1 The philosophical or scientific, concerned abstractly with the order of sciences or the order of things.

2 The pedagogic, constructed with reference to courses of education.

3 The encyclopaedic, closely resembling the pedagogic but including some material as well as the outline.

It is interesting to see that the earlier general encyclopaedias were arranged systematically by a classification of knowledge. Modern productions have suffered from the disintegrating effect of alphabetical arrangement.

Practical systems Richardson divided into the bibliothetic, for arranging books on the shelves of a library; and the bibliographic, suitable for arrangement of titles in a bibliography or catalogue and thus more flexible than the bibliothetic.

It is more usual today to use the term ' bibliographic ' to cover both of these functions.

THE UNIVERSE OF KNOWLEDGE IS A FOUNDATION STUDY FOR LIBRARIANS

UNIVERSE OF KNOWLEDGE is the name now given to the study of knowledge from various viewpoints as a preparation for the more technical studies of librarians. The study was initiated by the great Indian librarian and teacher, Dr S R Ranganathan, and is now being developed in several library schools in India and Great Britain. The most important elements of this study are historical, philosophical, and sociological. It is thus a field of knowledge as defined by Professor Hirst. The term ' knowledge ' is here used in its widest possible sense. It includes not only those disciplines that make statements about the world, such as science, philosophy and history, but also those that create such as the arts, crafts and professions.

The librarian *qua* librarian is not an expert on the universe of knowledge: that is the province of philosophers, scientists and historians. He is, however, interested in their findings and on these must base his own work in the organisation of knowledge. To distinguish the work of librarians in defining areas of knowledge for bibliographic classifications Dr Ranganathan has introduced the term UNIVERSE OF SUBJECTS.

READINGS FOR PART TWO

1 *Philosophical classification*

Adler, Mortimer (*ed*): *The great ideas*. Encyclopaedia Britannica, 1952, 2 vols (pp 888-889).

Bennett, J G: *The crisis in human affairs*. Hodder & Stoughton, 1948 (chapter 5).

Flint, Robert: *Philosophy as scientia scientiarum*. Blackwood, 1904 (pp 41-63).

Machlup, F: *The production and distribution of knowledge in the United States*. Princeton University Press, 1962 (pp 13-43).

Randall, J H and Buchler, J: *Philosophy: an introduction*. New York, Barnes & Noble, 1942 (chapter 5 'The basic methods of inquiry ').

Ranganathan, S R: *Prolegomena to library classification*. Library Association, 2nd ed 1951 (pp 392-393).

2 *Fundamental disciplines*

Hirst, Paul: 'Liberal education and the nature of knowledge', pp 113-138 *in* Archambault, R D (*ed*): *Philosophical analysis and education*. Routledge and Kegan Paul, 1965.

Hirst, Paul: 'Educational theory', chapter 2 *in* Tibble, J W (*ed*): *The study of education*. Routledge and Kegan Paul, 1966.

Kaiser, C H: *An Essay on method*. Port Washington, NY, Kennikat Press, 1969.

Phenix, P H: *Realms of meaning*. McGraw-Hill, 1964.

Reid, L A: *Ways of knowledge and experience*. Allen & Unwin, 1961.

3 *The unity of knowledge*

Collingwood, R G: *Speculum mentis, or, The map of knowledge*. Clarendon Press, 1924.

Kapp, K W: *Towards a science of man in society: a positive approach to the integration of social knowledge*. The Hague, Nijhoff. 1961.

Lund, J J and Taube, M: 'A nonexpansive classification system: an introduction to period classification'. *Library quarterly,* vol VII, no 3, July 1937, 373-394.

McRae, R: *The problem of the unity of the sciences: Bacon to Kant.* University of Toronto Press, 1961.

Martin, W O: *The order and integration of knowledge.* University of Michigan Press, 1957.

Randall, J H: 'The world to be unified', pp 63-76 *in* Leary, L (*ed*): *The unity of knowledge.* New York, Doubleday, 1955.

Reiser, O L: *The integration of human knowledge.* Boston, Porter Sargent, 1958.

4 *Scientific classification*

Sneath, P H A: *Principles of numerical taxonomy.* Freeman, 1963.

5 *Classifications of knowledge; theoretical and practical*

Collison, R L: *Encyclopaedias; their history throughout the ages.* Hafner, 1964.

Richardson, E C: *Classification: theoretical and practical.* Hamden, Conn, Shoe String Press, 3rd ed 1964.

6 *The universe of knowledge*

Langridge, D W (*ed*): *The universe of knowledge.* School of Library and Information Services, University of Maryland, 1969.

PART 3
LIBRARY CLASSIFICATION: THE ELEMENTS

LIBRARY CLASSIFICATION MUST ALLOW FOR THE PHYSICAL CHARACTERISTICS OF THE STOCK

We normally collect books in libraries for the sake of the knowledge they contain and not for their qualities as artefacts. The most important feature of library classification is therefore its relation to knowledge classification. However, in arranging books (records, films, etc) we are forced to take account of their physical characteristics, which require additions and modifications to any pure knowledge classification.

These characteristics constitute the FORM of an item as distinct from its subject. Form tells us what an item *is*, as distinct from what it is *about*. We have already seen that subjects are of more than one kind and we shall now see that there are several quite different kinds of form. For most purposes they are of secondary interest to subjects.

PHYSICAL FORM IS THE FURTHEST REMOVED
FROM SUBJECT

This is the most obvious application of the idea of form and merely tells us whether an item in the collection *is* a book, a gramophone record, a film, etc.

Some less important characteristics related to the physical forms are those of age, place of production, frequency of publication and extent of distribution. They do not play much part in library classification but it is necessary to be aware of such factors if only to know when they should be ignored.

The most important point to be made about these forms is that exactly the same terms can occur as subjects. Obviously, there are books *about* books, *about* records and *about* films. Sometimes an item has the same subject and form. *The anatomy of bibliomania* by Holbrook Jackson *is* a book and it is *about* books.

Since physical forms do not affect the subject matter they contain, the terms ' book ' and ' document ' in the following pages may be taken to stand for any physical form.

FORMS OF PRESENTATION ARE DIFFERENT FROM PHYSICAL FORMS

Within any given physical form knowledge can be presented in different ways. There are three distinct groups of these forms of presentation.

The first refers to the symbols used for conveying information. These may be (1) *pictorial,* such as drawings, maps and plans; (2) *mathematical,* including formulae and statistics; (3) *languages,* such as English, French and German.

The second describes the method of *selection, arrangement or display.* There are many terms of this kind. They may be grouped roughly according to whether they indicate :

1 *Order*—alphabetical, chronological, systematic, etc.
2 *'Literary' forms*—lectures, essays, reports, etc.
3 *Reductions*—abstracts, excerpts, digests, quotations, etc.
4 *Collections*—encyclopaedias, readers, selections, etc.
5 *'Keys'*—indexes, catalogues, bibliographies, etc.
6 *Rules*—codes, standards, specifications, recipes, etc.

A few words like this have both a subject and a form aspect. For example, 'dictionary' implies the subject 'meanings of words in a given language or languages' and the form 'alphabetical arrangement'.

As with physical forms, the forms of presentation can also occur as *subjects* of books. We can obviously write *about* alphabetical order as well as writing *in* alphabetical order. We can write abstracts or encyclopaedias and we can write *about* them.

PRESENTATION FOR PARTICULAR READERS IS OFTEN CONFUSED WITH SUBJECT

The third form of presentation gives rise to the greatest confusion between subject and form. With such titles as 'Statistics for engineers' or 'Psychology for nurses' it is easy to see how the mistake is made. It is wrong, however, to say that these books are *about* engineering or nursing. They are about statistics and psychology. The qualifications 'for engineers', 'for nurses' do not affect the subject matter; they merely indicate that treatment of the subject or selection of examples are carried out with the special requirements of engineers or nurses in mind.

This form of presentation for a particular group of specialists is not provided for in all classification schemes. One scheme that does so provide is the Colon Classification, and Ranganathan has named the form BIAS PHASE (*ie* the presentation of the subject is biased towards a particular group of readers).

Titles similar to the two examples above may merely indicate a popularisation of the subject. Examples are: 'A layman's guide to science', 'The intelligent man's guide to politics', 'The intelligent woman's guide to socialism', 'Music for the man who enjoys Hamlet', 'Mathematics for people who wouldn't bother if they didn't have children'. This is one way of indicating the *level* of presentation, which is also conveyed by such terms as 'Primer', 'Intermediate' and 'Advanced'. These distinctions are not usually made in library classifications, though they are sometimes used in special circumstances.

POINT OF VIEW OF WRITERS MAY ALSO BE CONFUSED WITH SUBJECT

Somewhat similar in appearance to bias phase is point of view, but this usually refers to the *writer* of a document rather than its reader. An example would be ' The Christian idea of education ', where the ' Christian ' was an indication of the views expressed, rather than part of the subject specification. There is a complication in that the same title could also mean that the book *was* on the subject of the Christian view of education—not necessarily from a Christian point of view. It might, for example, be a criticism by an atheist.

The simplest example of point of view is ' Pro and Con '. For example, writers may be for or against smoking, for or against women's liberation etc. Point of view has been largely overlooked in writings on classification and is not explicitly provided for in any scheme. (The point of view table in the Universal Decimal Classification is sadly misnamed. It has nothing whatever to do with point of view.) It is possible that more use of it in classification would be useful, but the main difficulty is knowing how far to go since every book may in some sense be said to have a point of view. Unless this is made clear in the title (which is rare) it is difficult to identify.

THE FUNDAMENTAL DISCIPLINES COULD BE DESCRIBED AS INTELLECTUAL FORMS OF PRESENTATION

The only earlier writer who referred to fundamental disciplines in this way was Berwick Sayers. He called history, philosophy etc INNER FORMS, as distinct from the OUTER FORMS of presentation.

We have already seen that Professor Hirst prefers the term 'Forms of knowledge' to 'fundamental disciplines'. They are similar to forms of presentation in that they tell us what a book *is* rather than what it is *about*. A history of Europe *is* history (*ie* is written in the discipline of history), but it is *about* the events in the past life of European people.

The sub-disciplines are mixed in that they tell us both intellectual form and subject. A textbook of Zoology *is* science and it is *about* animals.

Again, as with forms of presentation, the terms can also be used to indicate subject matter. In 'Philosophy of history' the subject is history and the form of knowledge is philosophy; and vice versa in 'History of philosophy'.

The difference between forms of knowledge and forms of presentation is that forms of knowledge *do* affect the subject content, forms of presentation do not.

There is a further group of terms which refer to specific modes of investigation within the disciplines. It includes Research, experiment, case study, questionnaire, etc. These too can describe form *or* subject. For example, we could write a book *about* the use of case studies in teaching management or we could write a book about management *in the form of* case studies.

CAN WE USE ONE SUBJECT CLASSIFICATION FOR ALL LIBRARY PURPOSES?

Subject matter is our main concern in library classification. The first question to be asked is whether one classification of subjects will serve all library purposes—arrangement of stock, irrespective of form; arrangement of catalogues, indexes and bibliographies; arrangement of general libraries and special libraries?

Opinion is divided on this question. Some writers maintain that a library classification can and should be made to serve all purposes. Others maintain that different schemes are needed for different purposes. Ranganathan is the most notable exponent of the first point of view, while the second is common in the USA. English opinion is divided.

The advantages of a single scheme for all purposes are obvious and attractive: economy of effort, cooperation between libraries and familiarity for users. Despite these, many specialists maintain that the way they see their subject and its relationships calls for treatment impossible in a general scheme. Two quite simple examples of this are Literature and Classics. Public libraries arrange literature primarily to meet requests for particular literary forms, such as poetry, drama or novels; academic libraries arrange primarily by period since that is how the subject is studied by literary scholars. Since the classics cover the whole life and thought of one culture they will be distributed throughout any classification scheme that is arranged by subject, but this would not be very helpful for the classics scholar.

There is also the difference between those who think that one scheme can and should be used for arranging stock and catalogues, and those who think that arrangement of stock calls for much simpler treatment than the arrangement of a subject catalogue.

WHAT IS THE RELATIONSHIP BETWEEN LIBRARY CLASSIFICATION AND KNOWLEDGE CLASSIFICATION?

Can we assume that, apart from providing for forms, a library classification is identical to a pure classification of knowledge?

The best modern thought says Yes, with some minor adjustments to allow for the way in which subjects are brought together in books. It recognises, however, that there is virtually no limit to theoretical distinctions that could be made and degree of detail that could be specified. It therefore sets a limit by reference to knowledge as published. This practical check is known as LITERARY WARRANT ('literary', of course, used in its broad sense of 'writings').

The term was originally used sixty years ago by the English librarian, Wyndham Hulme. He used it with a somewhat different meaning. He did *not* believe that library classification should be based on pure knowledge classification. He thought that the aggregation of subjects in books was so peculiar that it was impossible to fit them into the divisions of a pure knowledge classification. He gives the example of 'Heat, light and sound' as commonly constituting the subject of a book without corresponding to any division of knowledge. To him 'Literary Warrant' meant a classification system of the subjects of books, as distinct from philosophic or scientific classifications of knowledge. His point of view is still common in the USA. Hulme's argument was applied only to the subjects of whole books, not to the more specific subjects of periodical articles. Since his time, books have been written on more and more specific subjects and today it is difficult to see that the distinction is possible. Most modern writers would say that Hulme's point merely indicated that some adjustments were necessary to make a knowledge classification suitable for books.

'Literary warrant' is also occasionally used in the narrow sense of the *volume* of literature on a subject. It has been used in the Dewey Decimal Classification to set an arbitrary limit to the amount of detail specified in the scheme.

LIBRARY CLASSIFICATION USES PHILOSOPHIC CLASSIFICATION AS ITS BASIS

We saw in part 2 that philosophers are concerned with the kinds of knowledge, such as science, philosophy and history. Their analysis has practical application in the educational curriculum and in the division of labour. A theory of general education must take into account the various branches of knowledge. Teachers, scholars and other workers tend to specialise in the study or use of a particular body of knowledge. Practical distinctions are never as precise or thorough as philosophical distinctions, but we can see the similarity between them. If we are to serve people's interests, the same principle of division is an obvious choice for the basis of a classification scheme.

The principle has, in fact, been widely accepted and there is only one notable scheme that departs from it. The rest are divided into areas of knowledge called MAIN CLASSES. These differ in number from one scheme to another, are usually rather ill-defined, and make no distinction between fundamental disciplines and sub-disciplines. Nevertheless, most of them trace their ancestry to particular philosophical schemes.

The notable exception referred to in the previous paragraph is the Subject Classification, designed in 1906 by James Duff Brown for use in British libraries. It is also notable for being virtually extinct, and though there may be others we must suspect that at least one reason for its demise was its principle of organisation.

In part 2 we examined the difference between classification of knowledge and classification of phenomena. The Subject Classification used phenomena, more particularly the category of entities, as its primary division. On this principle, everything about sheep, for example, would be herded into one place—zoology of sheep, farming of sheep, butchery of sheep, cooking of sheep, etc. The obvious argument against this is that people are rarely interested in *all* aspects of a particular entity. It is doubtful whether there is anyone alive who is expert in zoology, farming, butchery and cooking.

Despite the general truth of this argument there is a more limited case for the grouping by entities within the fundamental discipline of Science. The boundaries between the individual sciences are no longer very clear and there is an increasing amount of interdisciplinary study. In the circumstances it may be time to abandon the old classes of Physics, Chemistry, Biology etc and to arrange scientific documents according to the entities they study—atoms, molecules, cells, organisms etc. This argument also applies to the social sciences, where it is probably even more difficult to preserve mutually exclusive classes called Sociology, Politics, Economics etc.

HOW MANY MAIN CLASSES ARE THERE?

Although the term main class has been used rather loosely, it usually means the fundamental disciplines (which are very few in number) and their major sub-disciplines, such as Physics, Chemistry, Biology, Sociology, Economics, Literature and Music. In the sciences there is a continuous tendency to more and more specialisation and the major sub-disciplines themselves produce offshoots such as Biochemistry and Geophysics. Ranganathan now uses the term BASIC SUBJECT to mean any area of knowledge in which a person might specialise. The term 'main class' usually implies about twenty or thirty areas of knowledge, but the number of basic subjects would run into hundreds.

Whether the areas of knowledge are large or small, whether there are ten or a thousand, the principle is unchanged. We must always distinguish between this process of dividing knowledge into disciplines and sub-disciplines on the one hand and specifying the phenomena that they study on the other.

LIBRARY CLASSIFICATION USES SCIENTIFIC CLASSIFICATION WITHIN PARTICULAR MAIN CLASSES

Having defined certain areas of knowledge we must now deal with the phenomena within each. Some of this work has already been done by scientists. We can go to zoologists for a classification of animals, to botanists for plants, to geologists for rocks and to sociologists for social groups. Such classifications of homogeneous groups of objects will demonstrate the use of the genus/species relationship. This is often shown in the following form:

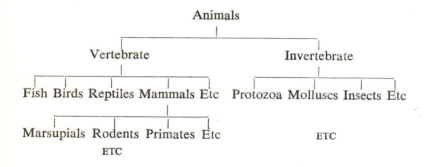

Scientific classifications of natural phenomena, based on the genus/species relationship, form only a part of a library classification. There are many other relationships to be found in the whole range of subjects of documents. They include the relationships of a part to the whole, a property to its possessor, an action to its patient or agent and so on. We must therefore look beyond scientific and logical classification for further principles.

An earlier theory of library classification suggested that given a particular area of knowledge we could divide it into successively narrower classes by means of the genus/species relationship. This is impossible since the genus/species relationship applies only *within* a given category. Our first principle for the classification of phenomena must therefore be the application of categories.

The most general set used for this purpose is that of Ranganathan's Colon Classification. It consists of five categories called Personality, Matter, Energy, Space and Time (frequently referred to as PMEST). Time includes any period limitation of centuries, decades etc. Space includes geographical divisions of continent, country etc. The others are probably more easily understood in the terminology of the Classification Research Group: Entity, Property, and Activity. (Ranganathan's Matter category includes both material and abstract properties, *eg* the wood of a table as well as its shape and colour.)

The use of the categories may be illustrated by (1) Library Science, where [P] is libraries (public, academic, special etc), [M] is library materials (books, periodicals etc) and [E] is library practices such as cataloguing and classification (2) Engineering, where [P] is the end product (buildings, bridges, machinery etc), [M] is materials (metal, wood, plastic etc) and [E] is engineering operations (designing, constructing, testing etc) (3) Sculpture, where [P] is style (Italian etc) and kind (busts etc) of sculpture, [M] is material (stone etc) and [E] is activities of the sculptor (modelling etc.)

The advantage of this set is that it can be applied to all areas of knowledge. More detailed sets are likely to have a more limited use. For example, the following might be used in science and technology: Substance (product)/Organ or part/Constituent/Structure/Shape/Property/Raw material/Action/Operation/Process/Agent/Space/Time. This is *not incompatible* with the first set, however, since any one of these categories could be allocated to the broader categories of Personality, Matter and Energy. Products, parts and agents are Personality; Constituent, structure, shape, property and raw material are all Matter; Action, operation and process are Energy.

Categories for use in the whole, or a large part, of knowledge are known as FUNDAMENTAL CATEGORIES. In the context of a particular class we use the term FACET. For example, we talk of the personality facet in the agriculture class. The particular principle used to define any facet is known as its CHARACTERISTIC OF DIVISION. In the personality facet of agriculture the characteristic of division is Crop. Wheat, rice, barley, etc, are all included because they share the common characteristic of being crops.

In other words, we use the term 'categories' when referring to the general structure of a classification scheme, 'facets' when referring to the manifestation of these categories in different classes.

More recently, Ranganathan has preferred to define facets as belonging to subjects of documents rather than to classes. For example, in analysing the subject of a book on the 'Economics of railways in Great Britain in the 1960s' we should refer to 'Economics' as the main class facet, 'railways' as the personality facet, 'Great Britain' as the space facet and '1960s' as the time facet.

In practice there need be no confusion if the term 'facet' is used in both senses.

SUBJECTS OF DOCUMENTS MAY HAVE ANY NUMBER OF FACETS

Despite the differences we have seen to exist between disciplines and phenomena, the term ' subject of a document ' is used in practice to cover both the area of knowledge to which it belongs (discipline, main class, basic subject), and the phenomena with which it deals. If it has only one facet it must be a basic subject, such as Physics, Biochemistry or Cybernetics. These are called SIMPLE SUBJECTS by Ranganathan, and they imply that the document deals with the whole field named and does not single out any particular phenomenon for attention.

Since our schemes are all divided first into basic subjects it is obvious that the names of phenomena alone cannot describe the subject of a document. ' Pigeon ', ' Toe ', ' Brick ' and ' Flying ' are all terms for phenomena, but they must be attached to basic subjects before they can describe the subjects of documents. Pigeons may belong to the basic subjects of Zoology, Animal husbandry, Sports, Cookery, Military science etc; Toes to Biology, Zoology, Anthropology or Medicine; Bricks to Building, Architecture or Chemical technology; Flying to Zoology, Aeronautics, Transport, Medicine, Psychology and so on. Such terms by themselves are called ISOLATES by Ranganathan, ie isolated terms, unattached to a basic subject. When isolate terms are listed systematically in particular classes they are known as FOCI within facets (ie from the whole facet we focus our attention on a single isolate).

For the subject of a document consisting of basic subject plus one or more isolates (eg Psychology of children, Economics of the motor industry in USA) Ranganathan uses the term COMPOUND SUBJECT. English usage has somewhat confused the issue by using ' Compound Subject ' to mean basic subject plus *two* or more isolates, thus leaving ' simple subject ' to include basic subject plus one isolate as well as basic subject alone (eg ' Psychology of children ' as well as ' Psychology ').

Further confusion is often caused by the use of ' complex ' or ' composite ' as synonyms for ' compound '. In Ranganathan's terminology both of these words have other uses. Complex is merely a special kind of compound and its definition may be found in Ranganathan's writings. 'Composite', on the other hand, does not refer to subject at all, but to books. A COMPOSITE BOOK is one that contains two or more *distinct* subjects.

COMPOUND SUBJECTS ARE PECULIAR TO LIBRARY CLASSIFICATION

Compound subjects do not occur in scientific or philosophic classification. Scientists and philosophers deal with only one category of concepts at a time and they are thus adequately served by the rules of logical division. In classification of documents we must deal with more than one category at a time, since the subject of a document may consist of a basic subject plus several concepts from different categories. A philosophic or scientific classification consists of single concepts such as science, history and philosophy, or rats, mice and guinea pigs. A library classification on the other hand must include such classes as 'Population characteristics of house mice living in English corn ricks'.

There are two ways in which we may attempt to achieve this end. The first is to list every possible subject, simple and compound that could occur. Older library classifications did attempt this (or something near it) but always failed dismally in the attempt. The number of compound subjects in documents is so high that the aim is quite impossible of achievement. Schemes that list a large number of compound subjects are known as ENUMERATIVE.

This method has now been replaced by one that does work. This consists in listing only basic subjects and isolates arranged in facets, together with rules for putting these elementary parts together to form compound subjects. Such schemes are known as FACETED or ANALYTICO-SYNTHETIC. They analyse subjects into their component parts, which are then listed so that they can be put together (synthesised) as required to describe the subjects of documents.

For example, the schedules of Colon Classification do not include the subject 'Cataloguing of periodicals in university libraries'. Instead we find 'University library' listed in the [P] facet, 'Periodicals' in the [M] facet, and 'Cataloguing' in the [E] facet. Using the appropriate rules and notation we are able to construct the class number 234;46:55. This is constructed from the component parts as follows:

3

2   = Library science class
34 = University libraries
;46 = Periodicals
:55 = Cataloguing.

COMPOUND SUBJECTS MUST HAVE AN ORDER
OF THEIR PARTS

An essential quality of a classification scheme is consistency in use, and hence predictability as to the whereabouts of particular subjects. We must therefore assume that the constituent parts of a compound subject are always combined in the same order, otherwise books on identical subjects could be put in different places.

For example, in the class Psychology we shall obviously have a facet of persons and a facet of mental processes. Books with only one isolate in their subject, such as Psychology of adolescents, or Psychology of intelligence create no problem. 'Intelligence of adolescents', on the other hand, could either go with Intelligence, qualified by Adolescents, or with Adolescents qualified by Intelligence. And so for every subject containing both a person and a process. Subjects with three isolates could be ordered in six possible ways (1-2-3, 1-3-2, 2-1-3, 2-3-1, 3-1-2, 3-2-1) and four isolates would give us no less than twenty four alternatives.

Strict rules for combining the symbols which represent component parts of compound subjects are therefore essential if we are to avoid chaos in using a faceted classification system. They are known as the rule for CITATION ORDER (sometimes called Combination order, Facet order or, by Ranganathan, Facet sequence).

Various principles for choice of citation order have been suggested. The most fundamental principle is that of dependence. Ranganathan calls it the Wall-picture principle. For example, in the subject 'Treatment of diseases of women', the concept of treatment depends on the concept of diseases—unless we first recognise the existence of disease there is nothing to treat. Likewise the concept disease is dependent on women—diseases can't exist unless there is a body to support them. The commonest citation order is one of successively dependent concepts. The subject under discussion would have its parts arranged in the order Women—Diseases—Treatment. This order of dependence is sometimes referred to as STANDARD CITATION ORDER.

Other principles of citation order include the subordination of means to ends, *eg* Music—Physics of; the subordination of part to whole, *eg* Bicycle-wheel; the sequence Patient—Action—Agent, *eg* Infants—Teaching—Play method; and the citing of the more concrete before the more abstract as in the order Personality, Matter, Energy, Space and Time.

Choice of citation order is very important since it determines more than any other factor the arrangement of subjects in a library. It must therefore be based on the needs of users.

Those aspects of a subject that occur as subdivisions in various places are known as DISTRIBUTED RELATIVES. For example, if we use the standard citation order in medicine we shall find diseases as subdivisions of women, children etc, and of the various parts of the body. Furthermore, we shall find them also in the agriculture class, since cabbages can have diseases as well as kings—not to mention rabbits in the animal husbandry class.

LIBRARY CLASSIFICATION MUST PROVIDE A COMPLETE ORDER FOR ALL ITS CLASSES, SIMPLE AND COMPOUND

Logical division does not provide us with rules relating to compound subjects, nor does it provide us with rules for arranging classes in an order. In a theoretical scheme we need only be concerned with the analysis of classes and their relationships—not with their arrangement in any particular way. In a practical scheme for library use we must have an order for arranging the stock itself and the entries in a catalogue.

Citation order is only concerned with the order of constituent parts *within the subjects of individual documents*. It does not tell us how to arrange *different documents* in relation to each other.

The term generally used now for the complete order of classes is FILING ORDER. When referring more specifically to the order of items in the stock the term SHELF ORDER is sometimes used; and for the order on the pages of the classification scheme itself, the term SCHEDULE ORDER.

'GENERAL BEFORE SPECIAL' IS THE MOST ELEMENTARY PRINCIPLE OF FILING ORDER

'General' and 'special' here have a wider meaning than 'genus' and 'species'. In fact any subject that is broader than, and completely contains, another is said to be more general. Such relationships are sometimes called CONTAINING RELATIONSHIPS. They include (1) Main class or basic subject in relation to all its subdivisions, (2) Genus in relation to species, (3) Whole in relation to part, (4) Class in relation to its members. Insofar as this order applies to genus and species it is sometimes called an order of DECREASING EXTENSION AND INCREASING INTENSION.

Most library classifications attempt to preserve this principle of order since there seems to be an implicit public expectation of it. This does *not* mean, however, that in such a system each item must be more special than the one preceding it. Many items are neither more general nor more special than those adjacent. (For example, if we have a sequence of biographies of different people it is quite obvious that there is no question of a general/special relationship among them.) It merely means that wherever the relationship of general/special *does* hold between two items the general will precede the special. For example, a book on Music in general would precede one on English music; a book on Mozart in general would precede one on Mozart's operas, and so on. Where items are not in a general/special relationship other principles of order must be found.

70

MAIN CLASS ORDER REQUIRES A PHILOSOPHICAL PRINCIPLE

If specification of the kinds of knowledge is a philosophical matter so too is the relationship between them. The order chosen for any particular scheme is likely to reflect a prevailing contemporary view. What is loosely referred to as ' evolutionary ' order is an example. E C Richardson expressed it as: the order of the sciences is the order of things, and the order of things is the order of their complexity (*ie* an order in which the simpler precedes the more complex). J D Brown put it more succinctly in defining the outline of the Subject Classification as Matter, Life, Mind and Record (*ie* Inorganic matter, Living things up to animals, Man, and the products of his mind).

Henry Evelyn Bliss even argued, though not very convincingly, that there was a close correlation between the order of development in nature, in knowledge *and* in learning. He also used a subsidiary principle in arranging the classes of the Bibliographic Classification, which he called Gradation by speciality. By this he meant that disciplines more limited in scope should follow those with wider application. For example, Physics, the science of matter in general, should precede Biology, which is limited to living organisms.

An entirely different view of life and knowledge is expressed in medieval schemes which give precedence to the Bible and religious writings, or the Soviet scheme which gives similar prominence to the writings of Marx and Lenin.

THERE ARE SEVERAL PRINCIPLES FOR ARRANGING ISOLATES WITHIN A FACET

One principle that operates *within* a facet is, of course, the general before special order that applies to a genus and its species. In the personality (entity) facet of Zoology there will be a complete list of animals in which 'mammals', for example, will precede the kinds of mammals such as marsupials, rodents and primates. A list of isolates like this, arising from the application of one characteristic of division, is known as an ARRAY. There will obviously be a large number of such arrays in a classification scheme for all knowledge, and an appropriate order has to be chosen for each. Ranganathan has suggested the following possibilities for ORDER IN ARRAY:

1) Increasing quantity. (Musical compositions could be arranged in the order Solos, Duets, Trios, etc.) The opposite order is also possible.

2) Later in time. (Writers in literature could be arranged according to their date of birth.)

3) Later in evolution. (Living things could be arranged in this way.)

4) Spatial contiguity. (If we start at one point we can arrange the counties of England by moving from one to the next, or parts of the body from head to toe.)

5) Increasing complexity. (Machinery for any purpose could be arranged in this way.)

6) Canonical order. (This means a traditional order, such as Arithmetic, Algebra, Geometry.)

7) Favoured Category or Literary Warrant. (This is the limited sense of literary warrant meaning volume of writings on a subject. This order would give precedence to the subjects in the array about which most had been published.)

8) Alphabetical order (where none of the preceding methods is relevant).

THERE MUST BE A FILING ORDER FOR FACETS AS WELL AS A CITATION ORDER

We have seen that citation order refers to the order of combining facets *within the subject of a single document*. We also have the problem of arranging books each representing subjects from different facets. For example, our citation order would tell us that in a book on the development of thinking in children we should combine the facets as: Children/Thinking. The problem of filing order for facets arises when we have *two* books, one of which deals with all aspects of children (in psychology) and the other with all aspects of thinking. Do we put the books on children first or the books on thinking first?

Ranganathan suggests that the principle here is that the more *abstract* subject comes first and the more *concrete* second, the book on thinking before the book on children. This happens to be the opposite of the principle used for citation order and is therefore commonly known as the PRINCIPLE OF INVERSION. The main reason for this order is that unless it is followed there will be places in the scheme where the fundamental principle of general before special is broken. This does *not* arise from the relationship between the facets. It is precisely because facets cannot be more general or more special than each other that we have to look for this other principle of order. General/special and Abstract/concrete are two entirely different relationships. The general contains the special, but there is no question of the abstract containing the concrete (or vice versa). The problem only arises when the place of compound subjects in the filing order is also taken into account.

For example, if we did not use the principle of inversion in the Psychology class we should have the following order:

Child
Child/Thinking
Thinking

where the more special subject ' Child/Thinking ' *precedes* the more general subject ' Thinking .'

Although it is quite a simple matter, this principle always causes

3*

confusion to students and for that reason it will not be further explained here. At this stage it is enough to know that the filing order of facets is chosen in a way that will preserve the principle of general to special wherever it occurs in the scheme. The principle is explained in more detail in the textbooks of library classification.

METHODS OF SHOWING ORDER AND RELATIONSHIPS MUST BE DISTINGUISHED FROM THE PRINCIPLES

We have now discussed the various parts, relationships and orders to be found in classification. There are only two fundamental methods for showing relationships—by *juxtaposition* or by *cross reference*. A classification scheme proper uses the first method, with a limited amount of cross-reference to indicate relationships not shown by the main order. In a faceted scheme it is only the genus-species relationship within facets that is explicitly shown by juxtaposition in the schedules. In a subject catalogue arranged by means of a classification scheme (classified or classed catalogue) the whole range of relationships represented in the subjects of documents will be shown by juxtaposition.

When subjects are arranged by name in alphabetical order relationships are mainly shown by cross-reference, though some will be shown by *juxtaposition* wherever compound subjects begin with the same term. Such a list of subjects is known as a *subject headings list,* and when this is used to construct a catalogue the result is known as an *alphabetical subject catalogue.*

Subsidiary methods used to show relationships of subjects, mainly in classification schedules, are indentation, style, weight, and size of type.

ORDER IS SHOWN BY NOTATION IN CLASSIFICATION SYSTEMS

Notation is merely a coding device to facilitate arrangement of items in a classification system. The order itself is complicated and obviously no one can be expected to remember all of it. We need, therefore, a set of symbols with a *conventional order* which can be made to represent the subjects in the system. In the West this virtually limits us to the Arabic numerals 0-9 and the Roman letters A-Z (or a-z).

It is very important not to confuse notation with classification. Classifications are made with concepts. Notations are added afterwards and must always be treated as subsidiary. They cannot improve a scheme, though they can hinder or prevent its effective use. The full range of problems connected with notation would take a disproportionate amount of space in an introduction of this kind. Only the main points will be made here.

We must distinguish between the *functions* and the *qualities* of a notation. There is only one function that a notation *must* perform and that is preservation of the desired order. This is achieved by a set of symbols with their own conventional filing order (*eg* there is a conventional order of the 26 letters from A-Z). If only one set of symbols is used (*eg* 0-9, or a-z, or A-Z) the notation has the quality of PURITY. As we shall see, there are difficulties in using a pure notation, at least in a general scheme. In practice a degree of impurity is tolerable.

If we project this requirement of preserving order into the future it must obviously include new subjects as they arise. The quality needed for this aspect of the function is known as HOSPITALITY. A hospitable notation is one that allows the inclusion of any new subject *in its correct place*. Integral numbers are not hospitable since once a range of numbers such as 1, 2, 3, 4 has been allocated it is impossible to interpolate anything between 1 and 2, 2 and 3, 3 and 4. Decimal numbers are obviously much more hospitable.

A second function that a notation frequently performs is to act as a locating device or link between the catalogue and the stock.

This will happen wherever the stock is arranged by a classification system, but there are some libraries, or parts of libraries, in which stock is arranged by some other method. Catalogue entries must obviously show where the items referred to are to be found. This function does not call for any further qualities in the notation.

NOTATION MUST BE ACCEPTABLE TO USERS

The qualities referred to above may be called technical in that they are necessary if a notation is to perform its essential function. To provide a conventional order and to preserve it in the future a notation must be reasonably pure and hospitable. (The terminology of library classification is not without amusing aspects.)

The other qualities of notation refer to its acceptability by users and may therefore be called psychological. They are summed up by the term SIMPLICITY. A notation should be easy to read, write and remember. Purity is a psychological as well as a technical quality since readers must be able to follow the order of the notation. The other qualities are BREVITY and MNEMONICS.

Unfortunately there is a conflict between brevity and purity. The main determinant of brevity is the number of symbols in the notation, known as the LENGTH OF THE BASE. With numbers we have a base of ten, with letters a base of twenty six. The longer the base the shorter the notation will tend to be for most subjects. For example, with numbers we can represent only ten subjects with one digit and a hundred (10×10) with two, and so on. With letters we can represent twenty six subjects with one digit, six hundred and seventy six (26×26) with two, and so on.

A pure notation of numbers is the simplest, but gives much longer symbols for individual subjects than does a notation of letters. If we use both numbers and letters we get even shorter symbols, but we have now lost our purity. As so often in life we are forced to compromise. We must balance the arbitrary element introduced into the order by having two or more species of digits (there is no conventional order as between numbers and letters) against the enormous gain in brevity. Other factors affecting brevity are the amount of detail to be specified and the evenness of allocating the notation throughout the scheme.

Mnemonics (aids to memory) are provided mainly by ensuring that the same isolate is always represented by the same notation, irrespective of the context in which it occurs. For example, in the Universal Decimal Classification the place 'Europe' is always represented by (4).

NOTATION MAY ALSO SHOW RELATIONSHIPS

In addition to its obligatory function of preserving order a notation may also show some relationships within and between subjects.

In the first place it may show the facet structure of subjects. For example, in Colon Classification 6th edition the notation for Administration in British Universities in the 1970s is T4:8.56'N7. The capital letter at the beginning means 'Education' and distinguishes the main class (or discipline) from its phenomena, represented by numbers. The first number following the class symbol is the personality facet, here meaning 'Universities'. The colon introduces an energy facet, here meaning 'Management'. The full stop and apostrophe introduce respectively the place and time facets, here meaning 'Great Britain' and '1970s'. The symbols used to introduce facets are known as FACET INDICATORS and the best term for a notation of this kind is EXPRESSIVE (*ie* expressive of facet structure).

A notation may also show the genus/species relationship within facets. This is done by means of the decimal principle (applicable to letters as well as numbers) in which decimal division implies subordination of species to genus. For example, in the personality facet of Zoology in Colon Classification we have

9   Vertebrates
97   Mammals
972   Marsupials
etc

A notation that shows the genus/species hierarchy in this way should be called a HIERARCHICAL notation. I am here suggesting the most accurate and concise terminology. 'Expressive' and 'hierarchical' are used rather indiscriminately in the literature of library classification, and the student is warned of possible confusion. The two things are different and a scheme may do one without the other. Schemes like Colon Classification that do both could be called 'Hierarchical and Expressive'.

The distinction is particularly important since the expressive quality in a notation presents no problems while the hierarchical

does. Because of these problems many modern notations do not show hierarchy and are known as (simply) ORDINAL NOTATIONS. In the following sequence from the British Catalogue of Music Classification, the notation preserves the correct order but does not show the way in which the subjects are related:

ARW	String instruments
ARX	Bowed string instruments
AS	Violin
ASQ	Viola
ASQQ	Viola d'amore
AT	Plucked string instruments

READINGS FOR PART THREE

Bliss, H E: *The organisation of knowledge in libraries and the subject approach to books.* New York, H W Wilson, 2nd ed 1939.

Foskett, A C: *The subject approach to information. Bingley,* 2nd ed 1971.

Foskett, D J: Chapter on classification *in* Ashworth, W A (*ed*): *Handbook of special librarianship.* Aslib, 3rd ed 1967.

Grolier, Eric de: *A study of general categories applicable to classification and coding in documentation.* Paris, Unesco, 1962.

Hulme, E W: *Principles of book classification.* Association of Assistant Librarians, 1950.

International Study Conference on Classification for Information Retrieval, Dorking, 1957. *Proceedings.* Aslib, 1957.

Mills, J: *A modern outline of library classification.* Chapman & Hall, 1960.

Needham, C D: *Organising knowledge in libraries.* Deutsch, 2nd ed 1971.

Palmer, B I: *Itself an education.* Library Association, 2nd ed 1971.

Palmer, B I and Wells, A J: *The fundamentals of library classification.* Allen & Unwin, 1951.

Ranganathan, S R: *Elements of library classification.* Asia Publishing House, 3rd ed 1962.

Ranganathan, S R: *Prolegomena to library classification.* Asia Publishing House, 3rd ed 1967.

Shera, J H: *Libraries and the organisation of knowledge.* Crosby Lockwood, 1965.

Staveley, R *et al*: *Introduction to subject study.* Deutsch, 1967.

Vickery B C: *Faceted classification.* Aslib, 1960.

PART 4
LIBRARY CLASSIFICATION: THE SCHEMES

CLASSIFICATION SCHEMES MAY BE GENERAL OR SPECIAL

' General ' in this context means general as to subject coverage. Existing schemes have been made, consciously or unconsciously, for a particular era and to some extent for a particular culture. Theoretical, historical and critical writings on general schemes are confined almost entirely to discussion of subject problems. The possibility of those schemes handling adequately the knowledge of all times and all places is rarely mentioned.

General schemes are made particularly for public libraries, academic libraries and national bibliographies. Special schemes are made for those libraries that emphasise one area of knowledge or serve a particular group of people (often amounting to the same thing). Such libraries are never as limited as their names suggest. A management library would include a whole range of industrial, economic and social subjects; an education library is likely to include psychology, philosophy, sociology and the whole range of subjects that are taught in schools and colleges. Special schemes are therefore said to have a CORE subject (the named specialisation) and FRINGE subjects (with varying degrees of importance to the specialisation). In Library Science the core subject is ' libraries and their activities ', a closely related fringe subject is Bibliography, and less closely related are a variety of social subjects. Thus there is not as much difference between the requirements of special libraries and general libraries as might at first appear. For this reason many people would maintain that an adequate general scheme should be the basis for all library classification.

Special schemes are used in bibliographies, indexing and abstracting services, as well as in special libraries.

DESCRIPTION OF GENERAL CLASSIFICATION SCHEMES

There should be three parts to any general scheme:

1 The schedules. These list the various classes of the scheme which may be used to represent the subjects of documents, ordered by a notation.

2 The rules for use. These may be concentrated entirely in an introduction, or partly distributed throughout the schedules at appropriate places.

3 The alphabetical index. This is an index of classes in the schedules, *not* an index of all the subjects that could be specified by the scheme, and even less an index to what a particular library contains. It is for the use of classifiers, *not* for the use of readers. Each library must make its own index of the subjects of documents *in its own collection.*

The schedules may be analysed as follows:

1 General structure—the primary division into areas of knowledge, called BASIC SUBJECTS by Ranganathan. Basic Subject is a generic term which includes MAIN CLASSES (the major disciplines and sub-disciplines) and smaller areas of knowledge. Ranganathan has distinguished three of these. CANONICAL DIVISIONS are traditional divisions within a broad discipline, *eg* Logic, Epistemology, Metaphysics, Ethics, and Aesthetics within Philosophy. SYSTEMS are schools of thought or methods of practising a discipline, *eg* Montessori, Froebel, Steiner systems in Education; Allopathy, Homeopathy or Acupuncture in Medicine; Gestalt, Behaviourist, Psychoanalytical schools in Psychology. SPECIALS indicate a limitation in application of a discipline *eg* Industrial Medicine, Tropical Medicine, Space Medicine.

In addition to the special main classes there must be a GENERALIA CLASS for documents covering the whole of knowledge, such as general encyclopaedias. There should also be provision for documents in which a particular phenomenon is treated from the point of view of more than one discipline. An example is *The scallop,* published by the Shell Company in 1957. It includes eight contributions belonging variously to the fields of Etymology, Zoology,

Visual Arts, Heraldry, Anthropology and Cookery. All existing schemes provide for generalia, but books like *The scallop* can be satisfactorily classified only in Colon Classification.

2 Structure of individual classes—the extent of analysis into elementary terms (rather than enumerated compound subjects), the method of grouping by categories, the citation order, and the amount of detail provided.

Schemes are referred to as enumerative or faceted but these are really relative terms. Colon is the only completely faceted scheme, followed by UDC. Library of Congress is nearest the other end of the scale followed by Dewey, with the Bibliographic Classification about half way. The only *completely* enumerative general scheme is Rider's International Classification—a splendid anachronism of 1961!

Some phenomena are common to all or many classes, *eg* activities such as research, properties such as size. These are often listed separately as COMMON SUBJECT DIVISIONS. Also listed for use in any class are FORM DIVISIONS (essays, reports etc).

The following notes provide a very impressionistic introduction to the major general schemes. This subject is well covered in the literature and for more substantial information students are referred to the readings listed.

DEWEY DECIMAL CLASSIFICATION

Author: Melvil Dewey 1851-1931 (USA).

Publication: First edition 1876. Eighteenth edition 1971. Abridged edition (Tenth) 1971.

Use: Widely used throughout the world especially in public libraries.

Structure: The main classes correspond roughly to the fundamental disciplines of knowledge, viz 100 Philosophy, 200 Religion, 300 Social Sciences, 500 Science, 600 Technology, 700/800 Arts, 900 History. (400 Philology does not represent a fundamental discipline.) The order appears to be without any principle.

The scheme began as a largely enumerative one, but has slowly introduced elements of analysis and synthesis. The need for this on a much larger scale was not explicitly admitted, however, until the 17th edition of 1965. The detail is quite inadequate for specifying the subjects of all books likely to appear in a public library.

Notation: Pure decimal numbers. Partly hierarchical and occasionally expressive. Hospitality depends largely on the decimal principle and some mnemonics.

Rules: Inadequate to ensure consistent use of the scheme.

Alphabetical index: Except in the seventeenth edition, which had to be amended, the indexes to Dewey schedules have been good. They include many compound subjects since the scheme is largely enumerative, but they are constructed with economy and printed with clarity (as are the schedules themselves).

Evaluation: The pioneer scheme for the age of extensive education and popular culture. Wide use due to this time factor rather than intrinsic merit. Now an outmoded scheme that lingers on indefinitely through professional inertia.

UNIVERSAL DECIMAL CLASSIFICATION

Author: Out of Melvil Dewey by Paul Otlet and Henri La Fontaine (Belgium), Frits Donker Duyvis (Holland) and countless anonymous committee members (nationalities various) of the International Federation of Documentation (FID).

Publication: First edition (French) 1905. Later full editions in French, German, English (almost completed), Spanish and Japanese (in preparation). Abridged editions in some sixteen languages. Trilingual (English, French & German) abridged edition 1958. Third English abridged edition 1961.

Use: Special libraries throughout the world and particularly in Europe.

Structure: Main class structure as in Dewey Decimal Classification. Individual classes depart considerably from Dewey, and a large amount of analysis and synthesis has been substituted for the wholesale enumeration of compound subjects. Full editions have great detail for the classification of special subjects; abridged editions comparable in capacity to the other schemes.

Notation: Decimal numbers plus special facet indicators, with colon as a versatile relationship sign. Partly hierarchical and partly expressive. Hospitality achieved through large amount of synthesis and use of decimal principle. Fair degree of mnemonics, but excessive amount of redundancy. Difficult to adapt for computer use.

Rules: Makes a virtue of not providing any—aim said to be a flexible scheme that can be adapted to many circumstances. Consequently necessary for each library to provide its own set of rules to avoid chaos in application of the scheme.

Alphabetical index: Varies from one edition to another. Abridged English edition is poor. Contains many numbers not listed in the schedules, and omits some terms that are in the schedules.

Evaluation: Hampered from the start by a poor structure, it has continued to suffer from lack of a powerful controlling mind or a consistent body of theory. Developed piecemeal by special subject committees of FID. An object lesson in the dangers of (1) Voluntary work (2) Committee work. Quality of the individual classes varies enormously. 'Universal' in title refers only to subject coverage since it has never laid down rules for international usage. Consequently there are as many interpretations of UDC as there are users of it.

LIBRARY OF CONGRESS CLASSIFICATION

Author: Anonymous members of the staff Library of Congress (USA).

Publication: Each class in the scheme published separately from 1902 onwards.

Use: Apart from Library of Congress itself is used mainly in university libraries in USA and Great Britain. In recent years many American universities have changed from Dewey to Library of Congress.

Structure: Class structure based on Cutter's Expansive Classification (1893)—an early competitor of Dewey's classification and now virtually defunct. There are less than twenty main classes arranged in the order: Humanities, Social sciences, Arts, Science and Technology. There is no apparent principle in the order, as might be expected in a scheme that was prepared as a series of independent classes. Within classes a large number of compound subjects are enumerated and there is hardly any analysis and synthesis except for places. Alphabetical order is very frequently resorted to (which is the antithesis of classified order). Citation order (as implied by enumerated compounds) is not always consistent throughout a class. Despite the many volumes of schedules the scheme is incapable of specifying many subjects of books published today. Quality and detail vary from one part of the scheme to another. Much better in the humanities than in the sciences.

Notation: Clumsy mixture of letters and integral numbers. Neither hierarchical nor expressive and completely without mnemonics. Hospitality achieved by leaving gaps and some use of decimal divisions when gaps are filled. Impossible to adapt for computer use.

Rules: None.

Alphabetical index: Separate index for each class (no general index). Many important terms missing, and cluttered with unnecessary repetition of subdivisions as shown in schedules.

Evaluation: The most unsystematic of all the schemes, with frequent possibility of cross-classification. Product of the hardheaded practical school who seem to think that theory has no relation to practice. Like the Dewey scheme, is frequently defended by the comment ' it works '. Since there is no question of a scheme merely working or not working, but rather of working over a wide range of efficiency, the comment does not have much significance.

BIBLIOGRAPHIC CLASSIFICATION

Author: Henry Evelyn Bliss 1870-1955 (USA).

Publication: Condensed version 1935. Full edition 1940-1953. New edition in preparation, edited by Jack Mills.

Use: More or less limited to Great Britain and Commonwealth countries. Used by far fewer libraries than any of the other schemes discussed, but particularly favoured by education libraries.

Structure: About twenty main classes arranged in an order corresponding to the broad implication of the idea of evolution. The nature, order and arrangement of these classes is given greater consideration than in any other scheme. Detail within classes falls between the two stools of enumeration and analysis, but a wide range of subjects can be specified.

Notation: Mainly capital letters, with numbers and small letters used for common subdivisions. Comma used as facet indicator, hyphen as equivalent of colon in UDC. Partly expressive, but not hierarchical. Hospitality achieved by decimal principle and ordinal notation (*ie* no attempt to show hierarchy).

Rules: Inadequate for consistent use of the auxiliary tables for compound subjects. Since the scheme abounds in alternatives it is also necessary for the user to decide very carefully which alternative to use in each case.

Alphabetical index: Not particularly good, with much redundancy through repetition of subdivisions already displayed in the schedules.

Evaluation: In conception and outline, this is the most scholarly of all the general schemes—the fine flower of the period of enumerative classifications. Unfortunately the detail within classes is not so satisfactory and Bliss left many loose ends in the methods for making compound subjects. These faults should be corrected in the forthcoming edition.

Bliss probably owed more to James Duff Brown than to any other previous maker of schemes. Brown's Subject Classification showed a similar general order, which he expressed as Matter, Life, Mind and Record. Bliss also makes some use of the principle of grouping by entities rather than disciplines, though the latter is his major principle.

93

COLON CLASSIFICATION

Author: S R Ranganathan 1892- (India).

Publication: First edition 1933. Sixth edition 1960. (Seventh edition in preparation.)

Use: Widely used in India for academic, special and public libraries.

Structure: About 40 main classes arranged in the order: Sciences and Technologies, Mysticism, Arts, Humanities, Social Sciences (History appears in the middle of these). Ranganathan's own explanation of this order is not particularly convincing. Individual classes divided further by canonical divisions, systems or specials where appropriate. Phenomena in each class organised by categories of Personality, Matter and Energy (Space and Time are treated as common subdivisions applicable to all classes). Citation order standard throughout the scheme. *No* compound subjects enumerated. The amount of detail in these 100 pages will specify more subjects of documents than all the volumes of the Library of Congress Scheme. Many schedules for the detailed classification of special subjects have been published separately.

Notation: Mixed letters and numbers plus special facet indicators. Completely expressive and hierarchical. Hospitality achieved by separation of facets, decimal principle and a large range of devices. Highly mnemonic and particularly good for use in computer.

Rules: The only scheme with a complete set of explicit rules.

Alphabetical index: Corresponding to the completely analysed schedules, the index refers only to elementary terms, never to compound subjects.

Evaluation: The pioneer scheme of modern classification and still the only completely faceted general scheme. In a class of its own for coherence and system, making it the easiest of the general schemes to use properly. Charges of Indian bias do not stand up to examination (there is far more Western bias in the other schemes). For various reasons has not been adopted by English libraries, but has been enormously influential in modern research, teaching and practice.

COMPARISON AND EVALUATION OF SCHEMES

Much has been written on this subject, though recent attempts at more precise methods of evaluation have been limited to special schemes. Experience of many years of comparative method in teaching practical classification does, however, provide strong indications of the strengths and weaknesses of the various schemes. There is more than one criterion of efficiency and more than one method of evaluation. Short of elaborate and expensive total evaluations it is perfectly possible to observe such things as degree of consistency obtainable in using a scheme, time taken in classifying items and range of subjects that can be specified.

One matter that hasn't been discussed in evaluation of schemes is the subjective or psychological factor. There can be no doubt that a person's fundamental psychological type will play a part in his preference for one scheme or another. This does not preclude the possibility that he also has good objective reasons.

Colon classification, for example, will certainly make the strongest appeal to the seeker of perfection. To the same person UDC will equally certainly be anathema—its whole ethos will offend every fibre of his being. This is essentially a scheme for those whose greatest satisfaction comes from achieving results in the face of impossible odds. Dewey is for those who are conventional to the point of timidity. Its long history and heroic resistance to change in the face of all needs gives comfort and reassurance (though admittedly its more recent developments must give them some cause for anxiety). Library of Congress is the practical man's scheme—for those who believe there are simple solutions to all problems as long as we don't think about them. The Bibliographic Classification will appeal to the supporter of lost causes. The years of sustained scholarship, seeking that elusive consensus of educated opinion, produced a view of knowledge that is far from generally acceptable.

For the past decade this group has examined the problems of a new general classification scheme. As a small voluntary group without finance it has not been able to make rapid progress. However, some important principles have been developed and tested. These include the use of certain fundamental categories, the theory of integrative levels as a principle of order within the entity category, and general systems theory as a framework for relationships between categories.

It is likely to be some years yet before any scheme is published as a result of this research. Much of the work to be done is lengthy examination of literature and listing of isolates within various categories, calling for financial support.

SPECIAL CLASSIFICATION SCHEMES HAVE BEEN THE CHIEF PRODUCT OF MODERN RESEARCH

The period from 1876 to approximately 1945 was the golden age of general classification schemes. They met the needs particularly of libraries catering for rapidly expanding education and leisure. Any special schemes made during this period were usually based on one or other of the general schemes.

Since the last war the emphasis has been firstly on the development of science and technology, secondly on social problems often produced by the so-called progress of technology. Special libraries and information services have expanded and the rate of publication has accelerated.

In England a Royal Society Conference in 1948 drew attention to the need for improved classification methods in science and technology. One result was the foundation of the Classification Research Group in 1952. Many of the original members were special librarians with practical problems of organising collections of detailed literature in various scientific and technical subjects.

For ten years the Group explored very thoroughly the problems of making a special scheme. Their methods were summarised by B C Vickery in *Faceted classification*. Schemes for particular subjects were produced mainly by individual members, though the Group as a whole was responsible for the Library Science scheme, through the sub-committee of D J Campbell, E Coates and J Mills.

Problems of special schemes may be considered in the three divisions of Science and Technology, Social Sciences and Humanities.

4

CLASSIFICATION SCHEMES FOR SCIENCE AND TECHNOLOGY

The physical sciences are in some respects the easiest subjects for bibliographic classification. Science is one of the most abstract forms of knowledge. It uses an artificial language with precisely defined terms which make possible the establishment of mutually exclusive classes. Categories and relationships are fairly easy to recognise. The complexity of reality is reduced to comparative simplicity. The sciences are also a very homogeneous group held together by a common method and subject (the natural world). This makes it possible to talk of the unity of the sciences in a way that we cannot talk of the unity of knowledge as a whole. We can generalise quite easily about classification problems throughout the whole range of the sciences.

Against these advantages we have to offset difficulties arising from the very rapid developments producing (1) more and more subjects for classification (2) very detailed and complex subjects (3) constantly changing patterns of knowledge. The literature of science as valid knowledge has a comparatively short life and classification schemes will be correspondingly quickly outdated. These generalisations apply to the empirical sciences and technology. Mathematics is a unique subject for classification.

A common error today is to treat Science as the paradigm of all knowledge. It arises from the influence of certain modern traditions in philosophy and the popular notion that science is steadily replacing all other forms of knowledge, or at least that it is by far the most important and superior form. These are highly questionable assumptions, and they certainly don't help in dealing with the problems of classification in other areas of knowledge.

The most accessible and comprehensive modern scheme is that designed originally by Jean Aitchison for use of the English Electric Company. Its latest edition has the title *Thesaurofacet*.

CLASSIFICATION SCHEMES FOR THE SOCIAL SCIENCES

The disciplines in this group have some similarity to those in the science and technology group. They use scientific method to some extent and they are held together by the common subject of Man. However, a good deal of the writing handled by libraries is not scientific and Social Studies would probably be a more accurate title for the group. There are many historical, philosophical and empirical elements as well as scientific. Since Man is by far the most complex of natural phenomena it is correspondingly difficult to make abstractions about him—to reduce him to mutually exclusive classes and precisely defined terms. The very nature of language (his chief defining characteristic) is that it does *not* consist of fixed meanings and mutually exclusive terms. Science is not the paradigm of knowledge in this respect, it is the odd man out.

A big difference between physical and social science is that in the latter much of the older literature continues to remain valid. It is therefore necessary to have a classification system that accommodates the different patterns of thought from earlier times as well as the contemporary pattern. A further difference is that where a physical science tends to be one agreed body of thought, in the social sciences there are variant theories, schools and systems of practice.

Even more than in the physical sciences, the boundaries between the various social studies are difficult to establish: there is an increasing tendency to make interdisciplinary studies of particular problems. This points to the possibility that a bibliographic classification for social studies may be better organised in what Paul Hirst calls Fields of knowledge (*eg* Urban development, The environment), than by traditional disciplines such as Sociology and Economics.

Bliss preferred the term Human Sciences for this group. The major disciplines included are: Psychology, Education, Sociology, Anthropology, Politics, Economics, Geography. It will be seen that Anthropology, Psychology and Geography have very close relations with physical sciences, while Education, Sociology, Politics, Economics, have strong links to Philosophy.

A good example of modern schemes in the social sciences is the *London education classification* by D J Foskett. It is at present out of print, but a second edition is in preparation with a similar plan to the English Electric *Thesaurofacet*.

CLASSIFICATION SCHEMES FOR THE HUMANITIES

The term humanities is here used in a wide sense to indicate all the arts as well as history, religion and philosophy. It is obviously not a homogeneous group in the way that the other two are, but the various disciplines do have some characteristics in common.

R G Collingwood, the philosopher and historian, asserted that Science can observe only the externals of human behaviour; Wilson Knight, the literary scholar, made a similar point in saying that no science understands the body-mind complex. The sciences are all abstractions from reality; the humanities are mainly concerned with man and the world in their concrete wholeness and complexity.

The humanities are therefore not given to classification as the sciences are; they do not make frequent use of abstract terms with fixed definitions. They are concerned much more frequently with individuals than with classes of objects. As W H Auden said in his T S Eliot Memorial lectures, ' The job of the arts is to manifest the personal and the chosen: the study of the impersonal and the necessary is the job of the sciences '. The arts are concerned with creation rather than statement, though studies *of* the arts in critical or historical writings *do* make statements. There is thus a distinction between the products of the arts and the writings about those products. In the sciences librarians are usually concerned only with the classification of ideas, not with the objects they represent. Libraries contain books on tigers, but no tigers; librarians need not be able to tell a tiger from Eartha Kitt, or a hawk from a handsaw (at least, not while they are in the library). Librarians are not directly concerned with all products of art, but they do collect literature (as well as criticism), scores and gramophone records (as well as writings *about* music), and reproductions of paintings as well as art history and criticism. The two kinds of items tend to need different treatment in classification.

Humanities literature does not date as scientific literature does: art, particularly, is timeless. A classification for the humanities must therefore concern itself with the whole intellectual output of civilised man in these disciplines. The humanities have been given less

consideration than the sciences or social sciences in modern classification work. There is, however, a good scheme for music, designed
by E J Coates, *The British catalogue of music classification* (British
National Bibliography, 1960).

1 General Classification Schemes: Surveys

Bliss, H E: *The organisation of knowledge in libraries and the subject approach to books.* New York, H W Wilson, 2nd ed 1939.

Maltby, A (*ed*): *Classification in the 1970's: A discussion of development and prospects for the major schemes.* Bingley, 1972.

Mills, J: *A modern outline of library classification.* Chapman and Hall, 1960.

Sayers, W C B: *Manual of library classification,* 4th ed by A Maltby, Deutsch, 1967.

Shaw, R (*ed*): *The state of the library art. Vol I, Part 3. Classification systems.* New Brunswick, NJ, Rutgers University Press, 1961.

2 Dewey Decimal Classification

Batty, C D: *Introduction to the eighteenth edition of the Dewey Decimal Classification.* Bingley, 1971. (Programmed text. Also available for 16th and 17th editions).

Parkhi, R S: *Decimal Classification and Colon Classification in perspective.* Asia Publishing House, 1964.

3 UDC

Mills, J: *Guide to the UDC.* British Standards Institution, 1963.

Mills, J: *The Universal Decimal Classification.* New Brunswick, NJ, Rutgers University, 1964.

Perreault, J M: *Introduction to UDC.* Bingley, 1969. (Programmed text.)

Perreault, J M: *Towards a theory for UDC.* Bingley, 1969.

Wellisch, H: *The Universal Decimal Classification: a programmed instruction course.* University of Maryland, 1970.

4 Library of Congress

Birket-Smith, Kjeld: *Local applicability of the Library of Congress Classification: a survey with special reference to non-Anglo-American Libraries.* Copenhagen: Danish Centre for Documentation, 1970 (FID/CR Report Series no 10).

Immroth, J P: *A guide to Library of Congress Classification.* Rochester, NY, Libraries Unlimited, 1968.

La Montagne, L E: *American library classification with special reference to the Library of Congress.* Hamden, Conn, Shoe String Press, 1961.

Schimmelpfeng, R H & Cook, C D (*eds*): *The use of the Library of Congress Classification.* Chicago: American Library Association, 1968. (Proceedings of the Institute on the Use of the Library of Congress Classification, New York City, July 7-9, 1966.)

5 *Bibliographic Classification*

Bliss, H E: *A Bibliographic Classification.* New York, Wilson, 1940-1953. Introduction to vols 1 and 2.

Mills, J: ' Bibliographic Classification ' *in Encyclopaedia of library and information science,* vol 2.

6 *Colon*

Batty, C D: *Introduction to Colon Classification.* Bingley, 1966. (Programmed text.)

Parkhi, R S: *Decimal Classification and Colon Classification in perspective.* Asia Publishing House, 1964.

Ranganathan, S R: *The Colon Classification.* New Brunswick, NJ, Rutgers University, 1965.

Ranganathan, S R: ' Colon Classification edition 7 (1971): a preview '. *Library science with a slant to documentation,* Sept. 1969, 193-242.

7 *Classification in science and technology*

Aitchison, J: *Thesaurofacet: a thesaurus and faceted classification for engineering and related subjects.* English Electric Company, 1969.

Vickery, B C: *Classification and indexing in science.* Butterworths, 2nd ed 1959.

Vickery, B C: ' The classification of chemical substances: an historical survey ' *in The Sayers memorial volume.* Library Association, 1961.

8 Classification in the social sciences

Foskett, D J: *Classification and indexing in the social sciences.* Butterworths, 1963.

Kyle, B: ' Towards a classification for social science literature '. *American documentation,* vol 9, pp 168-183, 1958.

Education: Foskett, D J: *London Education Classification.* 1963.

Law: Moys, E: *A classification scheme for law books.* Butterworths, 1968.

9 Classification in the humanities

Arts: Munro, T: *The arts and their interrelations.* Liberal Arts Press, 1949.

Visual arts: Broxis, P: *Organising the arts.* Bingley, 1968.

Performing arts: Croghan, A: *Classification of the performing arts.* The author, 1968.

Music: Coates, E J: The *British Catalogue of Music Classification.* BNB, 1960.

Redfern, B: *Organising music in libraries.* Bingley, 1966.

Langridge, D W: *Your jazz collection.* Bingley, 1970.

Philosophy: Perreault, J: ' The classification of philosophy '. *Libri,* vol 14, no 1, pp 32-39, 1964.

10 The Classification Research Group

Classification Research Group: *Classification and information control.* Library Association, 1970.

Foskett, D J: *Classification for a general index language.* Library Association, 1970.

Foskett, D J: ' The Classification Research Group 1952-1962 '. *Libri,* vol 12, no 2, 1962, 127-138.

4*

PART 5
CLASSIFICATION AND SUBJECT INDEXING

CLASSIFICATION IS THE MAJOR TECHNIQUE USED IN SUBJECT INDEXING

The term 'indexing' is used in at least three different ways:

1) As synonymous with the organisation of knowledge in libraries. In this sense it includes author and title indexing and description of documents as well as all subject work.

2) As the act of recording the contents of a collection, in contrast to the act of searching the collection for required information or documents.

3) In its narrowest sense as providing an alphabetical key to a systematic order, *eg* the alphabetical index to the contents of a systematically arranged book, or the alphabetical index to a systematically arranged (classified) catalogue.

Classification is sometimes discussed as if it were solely a technique for arranging books on the shelves of libraries. In fact there is a school of thought, predominant in USA, that does attempt to restrict classification to this role, but this is a mistaken view.

What we have said in part 1 about the place of classification in life suggests that there must be a good deal of classification in any form of subject indexing. In fact, the only difference between a classified and an alphabetical subject catalogue is the method of arrangement. The classified order takes full advantage of classification to show the major relationships of subjects by juxtaposition and sequence. The alphabetical catalogue shows these relationships by cross-references but they must ultimately be derived from a classification system. Likewise the various classes denoted by subject headings are a product of classification; and the order of their components produces just the same problems of citation order as the components of a class number.

We must therefore be careful not to confuse the use of ' classification ' as a fundamental mode of thinking and operation with the use which implies a fully fledged system including final arrangement in classified order.

SUBJECT ANALYSIS IS THE KEY TO ALL
EFFECTIVE INDEXING

Before we can use any classification scheme or make any index entry for a document we must be quite clear what the document is about. Unless we start with a correct subject analysis it is obviously quite impossible to proceed to a correct class number or index entry.

It is not quite as simple and straightforward to analyse the subject of a document as to classify an object (allowing for the fact that objects vary in the degree of training required for their classification). If I come face to face with a striped animal in the jungle I don't have much difficulty in saying, This is a tiger; but books on tigers are not striped and they don't growl or spring at us. They consist of several thousand words between two covers with a title that may or may not include the word ' tiger '. Subject analysis consists in reducing these thousands of words to a very precise statement of the subject scope of a book. In this exercise it is the ability to recognise categories and relationships, the major elements of classification, that makes possible accurate results.

Titles certainly help in this task, but they are notoriously unreliable and rarely precise. On the one hand they are likely to contain redundant terms, on the other to be lacking important concepts for the precise description of the book's subject. It is always necessary to go beyond the title to contents lists, chapter headings and introductions to make an accurate subject analysis.

This process of describing a book's subject is known as SUMMARISATION. It is the most used form of subject indexing in libraries. If we go beyond the summarisation to list all or some of the concepts dealt with in a document we are practising DEPTH INDEXING. This is the form used particularly in individual indexes to books, in some collections in special libraries, and in indexes to scientific periodicals. The degree of depth indexing (whether one makes 10, 20, 30, etc entries per item) is known as EXHAUSTIVITY (*ie* how many concepts indexed). This must be distinguished from specificity which refers to the degree of precision with which *each* concept is described. For example, Rabbit could also be indexed as Mammal or Animal, but these two terms are less specific than the first. (The term 'specific' is also used of compound subjects—'diseases of rabbits' is more specific than 'rabbits'.)

CLASSIFICATION IS THE BASIS FOR ALL INDEX LANGUAGES

For most purposes it is necessary to control the language used for indexing—we use some terms and reject others. 'Index language' is the generic term for such controlled vocabularies. A classification scheme is an index language that will produce a final index arranged in systematic order. A subject headings list is an index language that will produce an index arranged in alphabetical order of subjects with cross references to show the major relationships. For either kind we must translate the subject analysis of a document in our own words into the controlled language (class numbers in a classification scheme, preferred terms in a preferred order for a subject headings list).

Ranganathan has emphasised that there are three distinct stages in indexing and that it is important not to confuse them. He calls them the IDEA PLANE, THE VERBAL PLANE, and the NOTATIONAL PLANE. Obviously, we shall be concerned with the third only when using classification schemes. Subject analysis takes place in the Idea plane—*which* words we use to express our ideas is not important. Choosing subject headings for an alphabetical catalogue, or constructing alphabetical index entries for a classified catalogue takes place in the Verbal plane.

The procedure for classifying a document is therefore as follows:

1 Subject analysis in one's own words	
2 Decision on an appropriate main class in the scheme	
3 Decision on citation order for the class	IDEA PLANE
4 Re-arrangement of subject analysis in appropriate order	
5 Examination of schedules of the scheme to find necessary concepts	VERBAL PLANE
6 Construction of notation for the concepts according to the rules	NOTATIONAL PLANE

Both alphabetical index entries for a classified catalogue and subject headings for an alphabetical catalogue may be systematically derived from the structure of the classification scheme used in a library. The procedures are described in *Subject catalogues* by E J Coates.

CLASSIFICATION IS ALSO USED IN SEARCHING AN INDEX OR COLLECTION

Collections of documents are usually arranged in a classified order. Subject catalogues are arranged either in classified order, or in alphabetical order of classes with cross-references to show relationships. The essential action in searching a collection is that of MATCHING the description of one's requirements with the descriptions provided of the items in the collection. This can be done only if we apply exactly the same process of analysis to the enquiry as we did to the contents of the documents. It is not as easy, since readers are frequently very vague about their requirements. This process requires even more skill in use of classification.

Matching is done either by human eye consulting entries in a catalogue or by various types of machinery from simple punched cards to complex computers. The machinery does not affect the *principles* involved.

In traditional classified and alphabetical catalogues, a full range of classification techniques is used for their construction. They are known as PRE-COORDINATE INDEXES since the constituent parts of compound subjects are combined (coordinated) at the indexing stage. In POST-COORDINATE INDEXES (usually referred to simply as Coordinate indexes) only elementary terms are included and very few relationships are shown. This merely means that the full application of classification techniques is postponed till the searching stage. The index language for post-coordinate indexing is known as a THESAURUS. It should show all the classificatory relationships to aid searching.

ALTERNATIVES TO CLASSIFICATION?

Failure to distinguish between classification as a fundamental process and classification as the full range of techniques used in classification systems leads to much confusion and misunderstanding. Even those who specifically attack the value of classification schemes often do so on a limited knowledge of deficient examples of them. When people talk of alternatives to classification, whether they are aware of it or not, they really mean alternatives to classification systems. Classification in some form must play a part in all subject indexing.

We have already seen that traditional alphabetical subject catalogues differ from classified catalogues only in their final arrangement, where relationships between subjects are shown by cross-reference rather than by juxtaposition. Newer methods of subject indexing mostly use much less than the full range of devices found in these two forms of catalogue.

At the furthest extreme we find the CITATION INDEX, which works on the principle that if a given document interests a reader any articles it cites are also likely to be relevant to his needs. It is thus a method of establishing classes of related documents without naming them. For this reason it is complementary to other methods rather than a substitute for them.

The KWIC (Key Word in Context) and KWOC (Key Word Out of Context) indexes arrange the titles of documents in alphabetical order of their key words (ignoring conjunctions, prepositions, etc). For example, the title ' Population characteristics of house mice living in English corn ricks: density relationships ' would have entries in the index under ' Population ', ' Characteristics ', ' House ', etc. This use of key words merely establishes classes defined by single words (many of doubtful use) without showing any kind of relationship (even synonyms). It is thus a very elementary and deficient form of classification, justified by its producers on grounds of economy in human effort and speed of production through computer sorting and printing.

Availability and increasing power of computers has led to other

experiments with AUTOMATIC INDEXING. These are all extremely
expensive since they depend on reproduction of whole texts, or
abstracts, in a form suitable for computer handling. Index entries
are produced through computer programmes based either on frequency of occurrence of certain words (statistical methods) or on
occurrence of particular kinds of words or phrases (linguistic
methods). Once again it is obvious that these are merely different
ways of establishing classes of documents.

We may conclude, therefore, that in the fundamental sense

THERE IS NO SUBSTITUTE FOR CLASSIFICATION

Adler, M: *How to read a book.* New York, Simon & Schuster, 1940. (Clarion paperback, 1967.)

Austin, D & Butcher, P: *Precis: a rotated subject index system.* British National Bibliography, 1969.

Bakewell, K (*ed*): *Classification for information retrieval.* Bingley, 1968.

Coates, E J: *Subject catalogues.* Library Association, 1960.

Fairthorne, R A: *Towards information retrieval.* Butterworths, 1961.

Farradane, J E: *Report on research on information retrieval by relational indexing. Part I—Methodology.* City University, 1966.

Gilchrist, A: *The thesaurus in retrieval.* Aslib, 1971.

Lancaster, F W: *Information retrieval systems.* Wiley, 1968.

Langridge, D W: ' Classification and book indexing ' *in* Foskett, D J and Palmer, B I (*eds*): *The Sayers memorial volume.* Library Association, 1961.

Ranganathan, S R: *Classified catalogue code.* Asia Publishing House, 5th ed 1964.

Sharp, J R: *Some fundamentals of information retrieval.* Deutsch, 1965.

Vickery, B C: *On retrieval system theory.* Butterworths, 2nd ed 1965.

Vickery, B C: *Techniques of information retrieval.* Butterworths, 1970.

Wilson, T D: *An introduction to chain indexing.* Bingley, 1971. (Programmed text.)

EPILOGUE

The preceding pages have done no more than introduce the main ideas of classification and indicate their place in library work. Classification and indexing are means not ends. Nevertheless, they demand skilled practice based on sound theory. The two must be developed together by the student. The techniques of subject analysis, use of index languages and construction of indexes must be learned by practice, but this must be supported by adequate reading. The lists at the end of each part of this book give a good idea of the nature and scope of the relevant literature, though they make no attempt to be comprehensive. Many more references will be found in the various textbooks cited.

INDEX

This index includes subjects, authors and titles referred to in the text. For further lists of authors and titles see pages 31, 44, 81, 103-105, 117.

Abstract and concrete, 68, 73
Activities category, 40, 61
Aitchison, Jean, 98
Alice's adventures in wonderland (Carroll), 21-22
Alphabetical order, 42, 72, 75, 91
Alphabetical subject catalogues, 75, 109
Analytico-synthetic classification schemes, 65
Animals: classification of, 17, 20
Aristotle, 40
Arrays, 72
Art galleries: classification in, 17
Artificial classification, 20
Arts: classification of, 101
Astrology, 18
Auden, W H, 101
Automatic indexing, 116

Basic subjects, 59, 63, 86
Bias phase, 52
Bibliographic classification, 23, 42, 49-102
Bibliographic Classification, A, 71, 87, 93, 95
Bliss, H E, 71, 99 *see also* Bibliographic Classification, A
Brevity of notation, 78
Brisch, Edward G, 17
British Catalogue of Music Classification, 80, 102
Brown, James Duff, 57, 71, 93

Campbell, D J, 97
Canonical divisions, 86
Canonical order, 72
Carroll, Lewis, 21
Categories, 40, 61-62 *see also* Facets
Characteristic of division, 28, 62
Citation index, 115
Citation order, 67-68
Class inclusion, 26
Class membership, 26, 70
Classics: classification of, 55

Classification Research Group, 61, 96, 97
Classified catalogues, 75, 109
Clothes: classification of, 9-10
Coates, E J, 97, 102, 113
Coding, 76
Collingwood, R G, 101
Colon classification, 62, 65, 79, 87, 94, 95
Colour classification, 10
Combination order *see* Citation order
Common subject divisions, 87
Comparative method, 95
Complex subjects, 63-64
Complexity, Order of, 72
Composite books, 64
Compound subjects, 63, 65-68
Concepts, 25, 28
Concrete and abstract, 68, 73
Connotation, 26, 27
Containing relationships, 70
Coordinate indexes, 114
Coordinate relationships, 41
Core subjects, 85
Cross-classification, 28-29
Cross-reference, 75
Cultures: classification differences, 38, 85
Cutter, Charles Ammi, 91

Decimal Classification, 56, 87, 88, 95
Denotation, 26
Dependence in citation order, 68
Depth indexing, 110
Dewey, John, 15
Dewey, Melvil, 89 *see also* Decimal Classification
Disciplines, 35, 37, 54, 57, 59
Distributed relatives, 68
Duyvis, Frits Donker, 89

Eliot, T S, 23
Encyclopaedias, 42
Energy category, 61-62

Engineering: categories in, 61
English Electric Company, 98
Entities category, 40, 57, 58, 61, 93
Enumerative classification schemes,
  65, 87
Epochs of knowledge, 38, 85
Evaluation of classification schemes,
  95
Evolutionary order, 71, 72
Exhaustiveness in logical division, 29
Exhaustivity, 110
Expansive Classification, 91
Expressive notation, 79
Extension, 26, 70

FID, 89
Faceted classification (Vickery), 97
Faceted classification schemes, 65, 87
Facets, 62-68, 72-74 *see also* Cate-
  gories
Factory stores: classification in, 17
Farming: classification for, 20
Favoured category, 72
Ferrière, Adolphe, 18
Fields of knowledge, 37, 43, 99
Filing order, 69-74
Films: classification of, 11
Foci in facets, 63
Food: classification of, 10, 11
Forms of documents, 49-54, 87
Forms of knowledge *see* Fundamen-
  tal disciplines
Foskett, D J, 100
Fringe subjects, 85
Fundamental categories, 40, 62
Fundamental disciplines, 37, 54

General before special, 70, 72, 73
General classification schemes, 85-96
General systems theory, 96
Generalia class, 86
Genus and species, 30, 60, 61, 70, 72,
  79
Gradation by speciality, 71

Hands: classification by, 18
Hierarchical notation, 79
Hirst, Paul, 37, 43, 54, 99
Hospitality, 76
Hospitals: Classification in, 12
Hulme, Wyndham, 56
Human sciences, 99

Humanities: classification in, 26,
  101-102
Humpty-Dumpty, 19

Index languages, 112
Index to classification schemes, 86
  Bliss, 93
  Colon, 94
  Dewey, 88
  Library of Congress, 91
  UDC, 89
Information retrieval, 23
Inner forms, 54
Integrative levels, 96
Intension, 26, 27, 70
International Federation of Docu-
  mentation (FID), 89
Inversion, Principle of, 73
Isolates, 63, 72

Jeffers, Robinson, 19
Jung, Carl, 18
Juxtaposition, 75

Kern, Jerome, 11
Key word indexing, 115
Knight, G Wilson, 101
Knowledge: classification of, 35-43
  in libraries, 23, 56
KWIC index, 115
KWOC index, 115

La Fontaine, Henri, 89
Library classification, 23, 42, 49-102
Library of Congress Classification,
  87, 91-92, 95
Library science: classification of, 61,
  85, 97
Linguists: study of classification, 24
Literary warrant, 56, 72
Literature: classification of, 55
Logic, 28-30
London Education Classification, 100

Main Classes, 57, 59, 86
  Bliss, 93
  Colon, 94
  Dewey, 88
  Library of Congress, 91
  UDC, 89
Matching, 114
Mathematics: classification of, 98
Matter category, 61-62

Medieval classification schemes, 71
Meredith, Patrick, 15
Mills, J, 93, 97
Mnemonics, 78
Modulation, 29
Molière, 15
Museums: classification in, 17
Music: classification of, 102
Mutually exclusive classes, 12, 28, 30, 98, 99
Mysticism, 37, 38

Natural classification, 20
Newspapers: classification in, 10
Notation, 76-80
 Bliss, 93
 Colon, 94
 Dewey, 88
 Library of Congress, 91
 UDC, 89

Order in classification schemes, 67-77
Ordinal notation, 80
Organisation of knowledge, 23
Otlet, Paul, 89
Outer forms, 54

PMEST, 61-62
Part and whole, 30, 70
Partition, 30
Paul, St, 37
People: classification of, 16, 18
Personality category, 61-62
Phenomena for classification, 35, 60, 63, 86
Philosophic classification, 24, 36, 38
 in relation to library classification, 57, 71
Physical forms of documents, 50
Physical objects: classification of, 17
Point of view, 53
Post-coordinate indexes, 114
Pre-coordinate indexes, 114
Presentation, Forms of, 51-52
Principle of division see Characteristic of division
Properties category, 40, 61
Psychological types (Ferrière), 18
Psychologists: study of classification, 24

Psychology
 of notation, 78
 of classification schemes, 95
Purity in notation, 76, 78
Purpose in classification, 21-23

Quantity, Order of, 72

Radio programmes: classification of, 12
Randall, J H, 38
Ranganathan, S R
 categories and facets, 61, 62
 general classification, 55
 indexing stages, 112
 order, 67, 72, 73
 subjects of documents, 52, 59, 63-64, 86
 terminology, 7
 universe of knowledge, 43
 see also Colon Classification
Relationships in classification, 41, 75, 96
 between disciplines, 38
 class inclusion, 26
 class membership, 26, 70
 genus and species, 30, 60, 61, 70, 72, 79
 main class and subdivisions, 70
 whole and part, 30, 70
Richardson, E C, 42, 71
Riders' International Classification, 87
Royal Society, 97
Rules for use of classification schemes, 86
 Bliss, 93
 Colon, 94
 Dewey, 88
 Library of Congress, 91
 UDC, 89

Sayers, W C Berwick, 54
Schedule order, 69
Schedules of classification schemes, 86
Science: classification in, 20, 26, 30, 38, 39, 58, 60, 97, 98
Sculpture: categories in, 61
Searching, 114
Shelf classification, 23
Shelf order, 69
Simple subjects, 63

121

Simplicity of notation, 78
Social organisation: classification for, 17
Social sciences: classification of, 58, 99-100
Soviet classification scheme, 71
Space category, 61
Spatial contiguity, 72
Special classification schemes, 85, 97-102
Specials, 86
Species and genus, 30, 60, 61, 70, 72, 79
Specificity, 110-111
Standard citation order, 67, 68
Subject analysis, 110-111
Subject catalogues (Coates), 113
Subject Classification, The 57, 71, 93
Subject headings, 75, 112
Subject indexing, 109-116
Subjects of documents, 35, 63-68
 in relation to forms, 50-54
Subordinate relationship, 41
Summarisation, 110
Supermarkets: classification in, 11, 17
Superordinate relationship, 41
Systems in a discipline, 86, 99

Technology: classification in, 97, 98
Television programmes: classification of, 12
Thesaurofacet (English Electric Company), 98
Thesaurus, 114
Time, Order of, 72
Time category, 61
Titles of documents, 110
Traffic flow: classification of, 11-12

Unity of knowledge, 38
Universal Decimal Classification, 78, 87, 89-90, 95
Universe of knowledge, 43
Universe of subjects, 43

Vickery, B C, 97

Wall-picture principle, 67
Whole and part, 30, 70

Zodiac, 18
Zoologists: Classification by, 20
Zoos: Classification in, 17